French Interiors FRANZÖSISCHE INTERIEURS

A
DOM
publishers

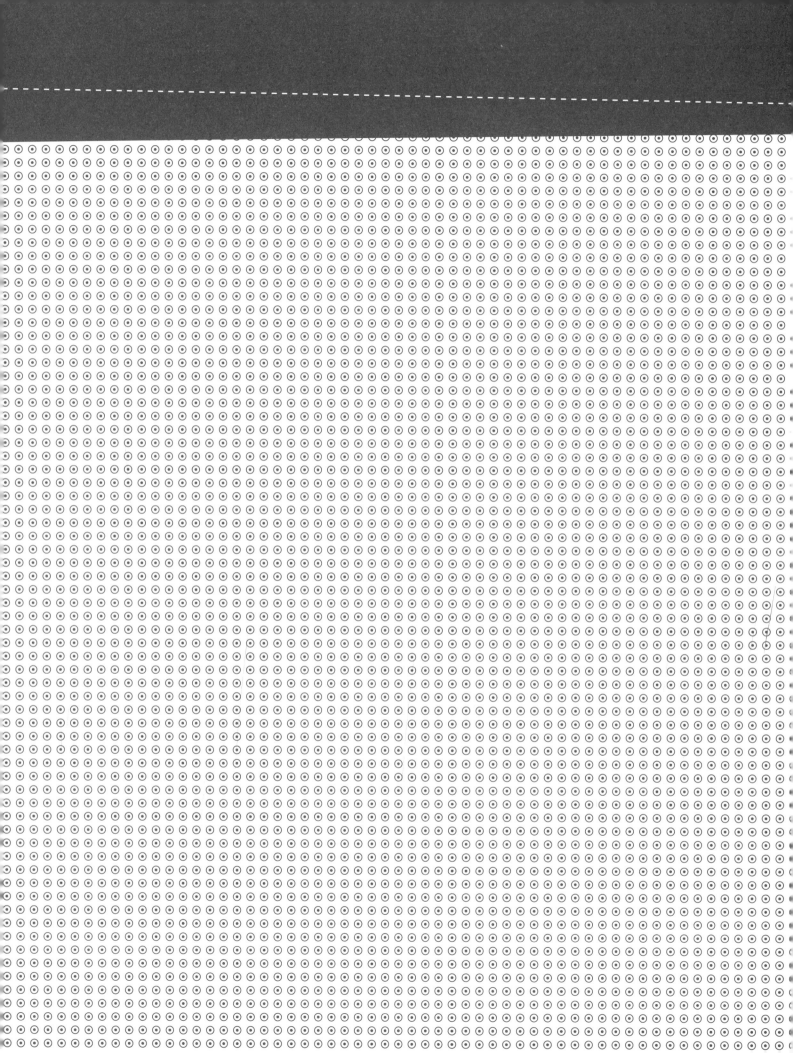

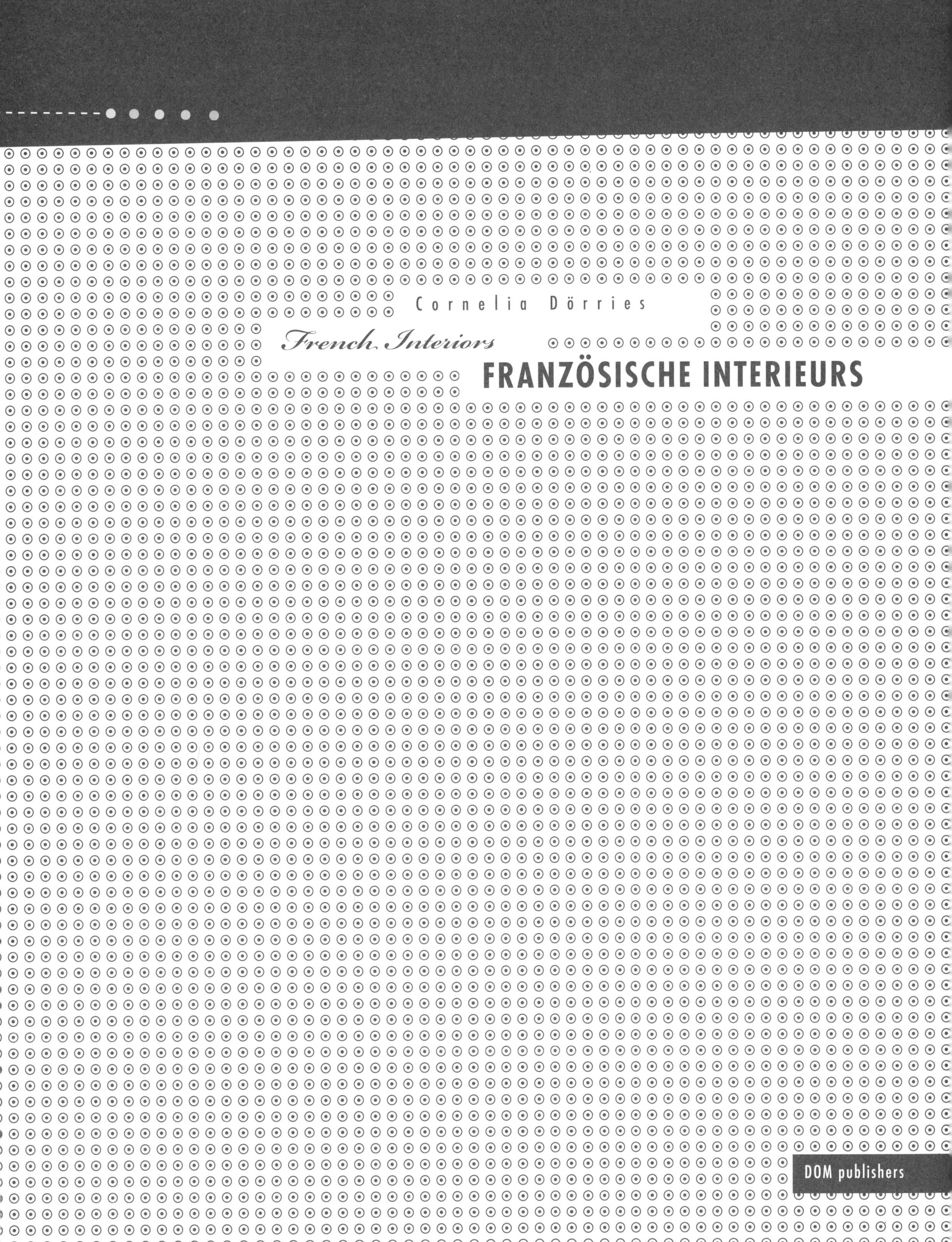
Cornelia Dörries

French Interiors

FRANZÖSISCHE INTERIEURS

DOM publishers

public space

arts and culture

offices and studios

shops and boutiques

entertainment

Court of Justice [Epinal [France [2001

Architect Rémy Butler [*Photographer* Patrick Tourneboeuf

Wie es sich für ein historisches Justizgebäude gehört, befindet sich auch das Gericht in Epinal mitten im Stadtzentrum. In dem kleinteiligen Kontext galt es, sowohl die Umbauten an dem aus der Ära Napoleons stammenden Bauwerk behutsam anzugehen als auch den neuen Gebäudetrakt auf der nördlichen Seite mit Rücksicht auf die Umgebung zu gestalten. Die Arbeiten erfolgten unter Einbeziehung der verschiedenen Ergänzungs- und Erweiterungsbauten des Gerichts aus mehreren Epochen. Für die Gestaltung der neuen Halle wurde ein Konzept entwickelt, das auf den Prinzipien von Klarheit und Ausgewogenheit beruht; mithin Grundsätze der Rechtsprechung.

Bei der Renovierung der Fassade fanden traditionelle, lokaltypische Materialien Verwendung. Der Vorplatz jedoch ist als kühl-modernes Raster aus Glas und fein geschnittenem roten Stein aus der Gegend angelegt.

Die zentrale Halle ist ein lichtdurchfluteter Raum, der die verschiedenen Dimensionen des Gebäudes bündelt. Hier treffen sich Anwälte und Mandanten unter einer sanft geschwungenen Decke aus Kirschholz. Von hier aus sind die beiden Gerichtssäle im Erdgeschoss zu erreichen, die in ihrer elliptischen Form wie Apsiden sowohl an der äußeren Gebäudehülle wie auch im Inneren wirken. Die Große Strafkammer wird von einem Lichtdach gekrönt, das als Symbol für die übergeordnete Bedeutung des Rechts in der modernen Gesellschaft dient. Für die Einrichtung der Säle wurden harte, verlässliche Materialien verwendet: helles Buchenholz und weißer Marmor.

As is proper for a historical building of justice, the court in Epinal is situated in the city centre. The intention, in the immediate context, was to approach the renovations on the building originating in the Napoleonic era with care and to design the new building tract on the northern side with consideration for the environment. The work then followed, including the various extensions and expansions of the court from different epochs. A concept was developed for the design of the new hall based upon principles of clarity and balance – and, consequently, upon principles of precedent case law.

Traditional materials typical of the locality were used in renovating the façade, while the square in front is designed as a coolly modern grid out of glass and finely cut red stone from the area.

The central hall is a room flooded with light, concentrating the various dimensions of the building. Lawyers and mandates meet here under a gently curved ceiling of cherry wood. Both courtrooms on the ground floor can be reached from here; their elliptical form gives them the effect of apses, both in the outer building shell and on the inside. The large criminal division is crowned by a transparent roof serving as a symbol for the higher importance of law in modern society. Hard, reliable materials were used for the furnishing of the halls – light beech wood and white marble.

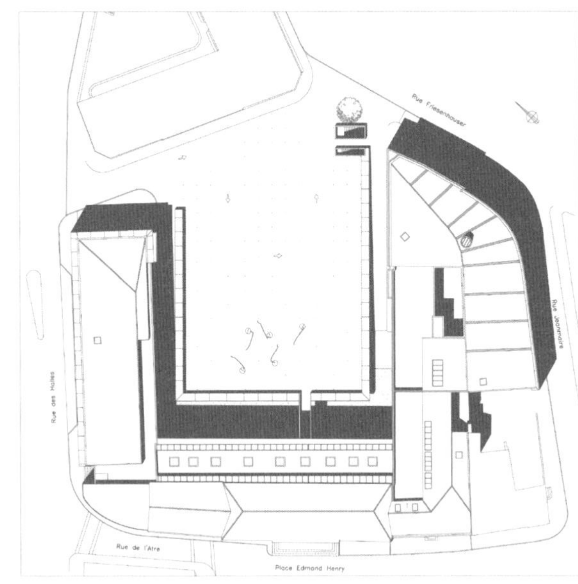

Links Gelungene Verbindung zwischen Alt und Neu [*Left* Successful combination of the old and the new [*Rechts* Die große Strafkammer [*Right* The large criminal division

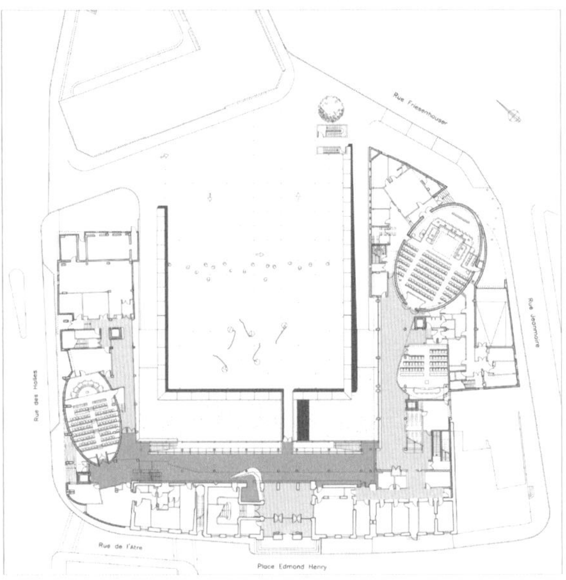

AUDIENCES
PENALES

République Française

Oben Historie und Moderne treffen in der Halle aufeinander [*Above* History and modernism meet in the hall

Child Centre – Hospital Care [Nanterre [France [2001

Architects Ameller & Dubois et Associés [*Photographer* Luc Boegly

Das neu erbaute Kindergesundheitszentrum in Nanterre besitzt aufgrund seiner hohen Mauern und des beachtlichen Volumens die architektonische Präsenz einer alten Festung. Mit dem recht unspektakulären städtischen Umfeld ist es über den angeschlossenen Kindergarten verbunden, der als eine Art Appendix an der äußeren Grundstücksgrenze platziert ist.

Während die Straßenfassade als introvertierte, dem Trubel der Stadt abgekehrte Front gestaltet wurde, die nicht nur eine beruhigende Eingangssituation evoziert, sondern auch das Gefühl von Schutz und Geborgenheit vermittelt, öffnet sich das Gebäude an seiner Rückseite zu einem großen, abwechslungsreich gestalteten Garten. Hier bieten bunte, kindgerechte Spielobjekte und unterschiedlich farbige Markierungen sowohl Ablenkung als auch Orientierung. Auch das Innere des Neubaus ist durch Übersichtlichkeit und Großzügigkeit charakterisiert. Ein zentraler, mit Kupfer ummantelter Korpus bildet das Herzstück des Gebäudes. Alle Ebenen sind stufenlos miteinander verbunden: Die Stockwerke gehen sanft ineinander über und sind auch für Kinderwagen oder Rollstühle problemlos zu erschließen. Bei der Gestaltung wurde auf nüchterne Rechtwinkligkeit verzichtet; stattdessen lebt die anregende Atmosphäre von schrägen Wänden, anthroposophisch verspielten Formen und einer angenehmen Farbigkeit.

High walls and considerable volume give the new children's health centre in Nanterre the architectonic presence of an old fortress. The adjoining kindergarten, placed as a kind of appendix to the outer property boundary, connects it to its rather unspectacular urban environment. While the street façade was designed as an introverted front turned away from the bustle of the city, evoking both a calming entrance situation and the feeling of protection and comfort, the rear side of the building opens up onto a large, variegated garden. Colourful objects suitable for children to play with and various colourful markings offer both diversion and orientation. The interior of the new construction is also expansive and easy to take in. A central body covered with copper forms the heart of the building. All levels of the building are connected to each other without steps; one easily moves from storey to storey, also with strollers or wheelchairs without any problems at all. Matter-of-fact squareness was dispensed with during the designing phase; instead the stimulating atmosphere is enlivened by slanted walls, playful forms reminiscent of anthroposophy and an agreeable colour combination.

Oben Der Flur erinnert an Mondrians abstrakte Gemälde [*Above* The corridor is reminiscent of Mondrian's abstract paintings [*Rechts* Klassisch modern auch die geschwungene Reihe der Oberlichter [*Right* The curved row of skylights is also classically modern

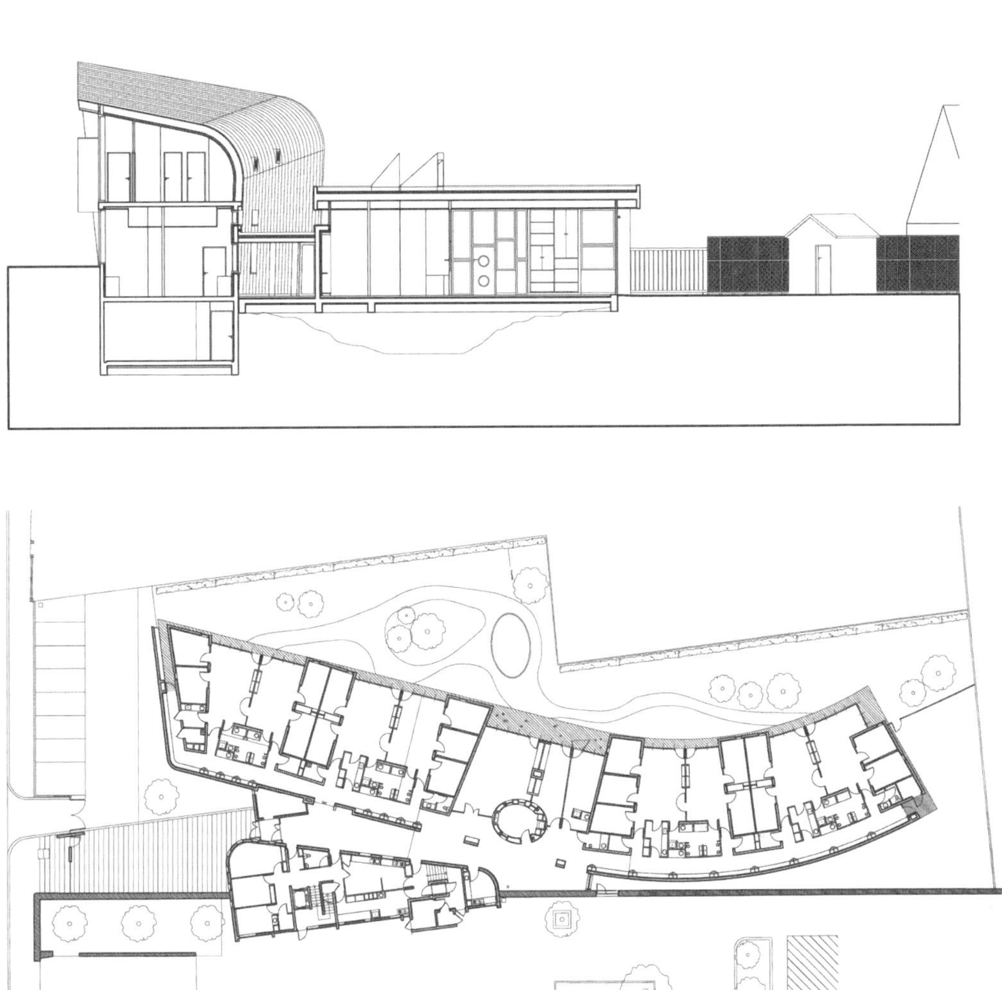

Oben Querschnitt, Grundriss, Längsschnitt [*Above* Cross section, ground plan, longitudinal section [*Links* Natürliche Materialien, organische Formen, fröhlich leuchtende Farben [*Left* Natural materials, organic forms, cheerfully bright colours

International Perfume Institute [Versailles [France [2003

Architects Ameller & Dubois et Associés [*Photographer* Luc Boegly

In der städtebaulich sensiblen Umgebung des Ortes Versailles befindet sich das Internationale Parfüminstitut. Auf behutsame, gleichwohl entschieden moderne Weise ergänzt der Neubau das bestehende Ensemble mit zwei Pavillons. Der Gebäudekörper besteht aus zwei gegenüberliegenden Quadern, die über einen Flachbau miteinander verbunden sind. In diesem Relaisstück befindet sich die Eingangshalle, von der aus die öffentlichen Bereiche auf der rechten sowie die Seminarbereiche auf der linken Seite zu erreichen sind. Das Herz des Gebäudes wurde für Bibliothek, Cafeteria und Konferenzsaal reserviert. Diese kommunikativen, für Besucher offenen Bereiche öffnen sich mit großen Glasfronten zum Park. Der im ersten Geschoss aufgesetzte, lang gezogene Trakt für Bibliothek und Konferenzsaal ist mit seiner Verkleidung aus Terrakottafliesen deutlich abgesetzt. Für den Seminarbereich wurde ein horizontal gestreckter Körper entworfen, der sich in die leicht wellige Landschaft fügt und mit Split-Levels im Inneren auf diese besondere Beschaffenheit des Baugrunds reagiert. Die Rückseite des Gebäudes beherbergt die Laborräume. Mit ihrer blauen Steinfassade bildet diese Front einen sublimen Kontrast zu den alten, hohen Bäumen, die das Grundstück begrenzen. Die zweigeschossige Halle, ein Laden sowie eine »Osmotheque« verbinden die einzelnen Elemente des Baus auf sehr sinnliche Weise miteinander: Hier setzen die Architekten auf das reizvolle Zusammenspiel von Farben und Materialien.

The International Perfume Institute is located in Versailles, a sensitive town with respect to urban architecture. The new construction completes the already existing ensemble with two pavilions in a considerate yet decidedly modern way. The building consists of two ashlars opposite each other, connected by a shallow building. The entrance hall is found in this relais piece, from which the public areas can be reached from both the right side and the seminar areas on the left side.

The heart of the building has been reserved for the library, cafeteria and conference hall. These communicative areas are open to visitors and also open up onto the park with large glass-fronts. The long extended tract for the library and conference hall in the first storey is clearly separated due to its terracotta-tile panelling. A horizontally stretched-out body was designed for the seminar area, joining into the gently rolling landscape and reacting to this special characteristic of the grounds with split-levels on the inside. The rear side of the building houses the laboratories. This front, with its blue stone façade, forms a sublime contrast to the old, tall tress bordering on the property. The two-storey hall, a shop and an »Osmotheque« connect the individual elements of the building in a very sensual way; the architects make the most here out of the stimulating interplay between colours and materials.

Oben Nüchtern und klar: Treppenhaus und Foyer [*Above* Clear and functional: stairway and foyer [*Rechts* Durchsicht zum Park [*Right* View onto the park

Links Präsentationsraum [*Left* Presentation room [*Rechts* Weg durch den kleinen Park | Grundrisse Erdgeschoss und 1. Obergeschoss [*Right* Path through the small park [Plans of the ground floor and first storey

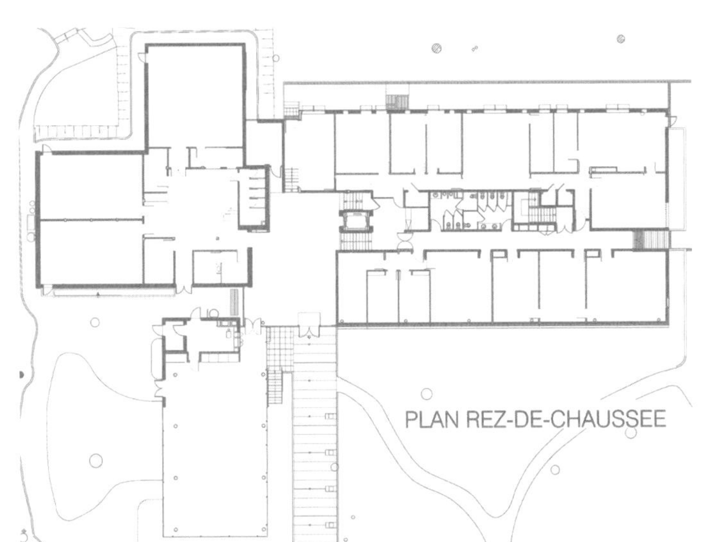

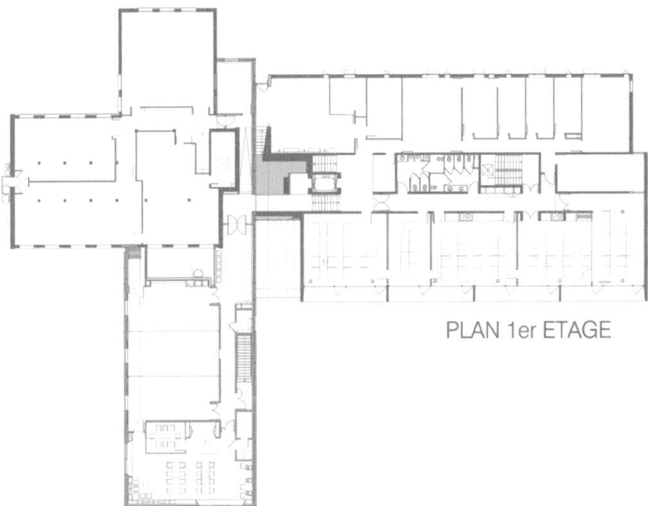

Ambassade de France [Berlin [Germany [2002

Architect Christian de Portzamparc [*Photographer* Philipp Meuser

Der Palast als räumliche Einheit von öffentlicher Macht und privater Existenz stand bei der Errichtung der Französischen Botschaft am Pariser Platz in Berlin Pate; und diesem traditionellen Konzept ist es auch zu verdanken, dass der Neubau Residenz und Konsulat unter einem Dach an historischer Stelle vereint. Das Grundstück am Brandenburger Tor wurde weiland von Napoleon III. erworben und diente bis zum Zweiten Weltkrieg als Sitz des französischen Gesandten. Die Ruine des 1945 zerstörten barocken Stadtpalais wurde 1959 abgetragen; die Adresse verschwand aus dem Bewusstsein der geteilten Stadt, denn der Pariser Platz war bis zum Fall der Mauer ein leeres Niemandsland zwischen verfeindeten Systemen. Von diesen Verwerfungen der Weltgeschichte hat sich der Ort überraschend schnell erholt. Den schönsten Blick auf das Geviert zwischen Hotel Adlon und Quadriga genießt ohne Zweifel der französische Botschafter. Seine Räume, im Westteil des Gebäudes gelegen, bieten eine großartige Aussicht auf das vornehme Ensemble moderner und historischer Bauten. Die Fenster zum Garten mit Birken und Robinien werden nur einmal im Jahr geöffnet: am 14. Juli, dem französischen Nationalfeiertag. Schöner Eklektizismus prägt auch das Interieur der Residenz: Antike Bauelemente, moderne Kunst und die sagenhafte französische Eleganz wurden auf eine Weise vereint, die dem Gast Bewunderung und Ehrfurcht abnötigt. Noblesse oblige.

The Palace as a spatial unity of public power and private existence sponsored the construction of the French Embassy on Pariser Platz in Berlin; it is also thanks to this traditional concept that the new construction unites residence and consulate under the same roof at an historical location. The property at the Brandenburg Gate was formerly acquired by Napoleon III and served as the seat of the French envoy until the Second World War. The ruins of the baroque City Palace, destroyed in 1945, were cleared away in 1959; the address disappeared from the consciousness of the divided city, for Pariser Platz was an empty no-man's land between antagonistic systems until the fall of the Wall. The location's recovery from these faults of world history was surprisingly rapid. The French Ambassador doubtless enjoys the finest view onto the square between the Hotel Adlon and the Quadriga. His rooms, located in the western part of the building, offer a magnificent view onto the noble ensemble of modern and historical buildings. The windows to the garden with birches and robinias are only opened once a year – on 14 July, the French National Holiday. Beautiful eclecticism also marks the interior of the residence. Antique constructional elements, modern art and legendary French elegance have been unified in a manner which commands the guest's admiration and respect. Noblesse oblige.

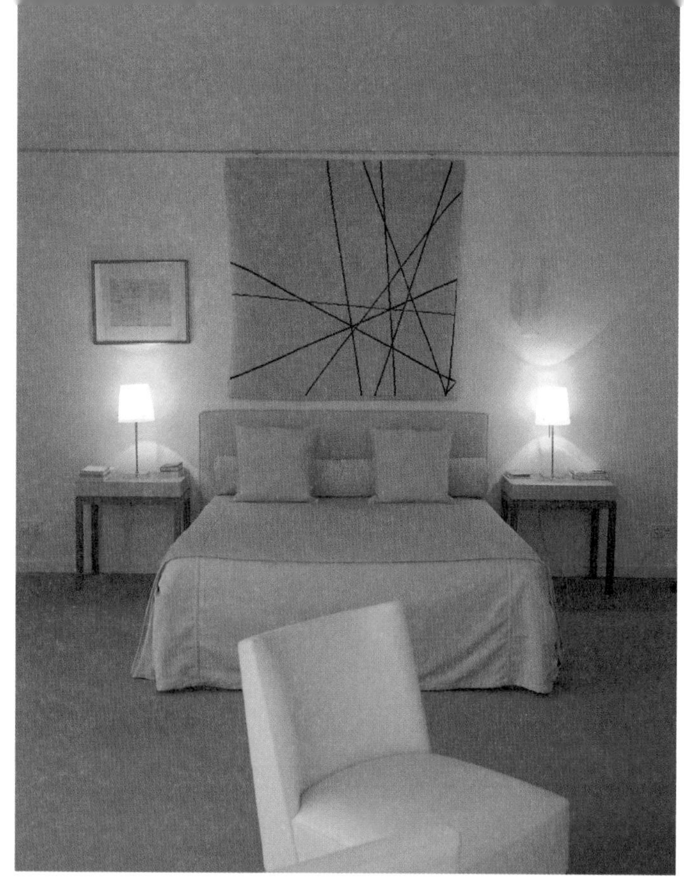

Links/Rechts Behagliche Wärme in den Privaträumen, kühle Eleganz in den öffentlichen Bereichen
Left/Right Comfortable warmth in the private rooms, cool elegance in the public area

Links Foyer [*Left* Foyer [*Rechts* Großer Empfangssalon, im Hintergrund die Bibliothek [*Right* Large reception salon, the library in the background

Cultural Centre [Saint-Louis [France [2000

Architect Manuelle Gautrand [*Photographer* Philippe Ruault

Der Neubau eines Kulturzentrums war Teil einer umfassenden Restrukturierung und Modernisierung der Innenstadt von Saint-Louis, einem kleinen Ort an der französisch-schweizerischen Grenze nahe Basel. Das Gebäude fasst neben einem Multiplexkino auch ein Theater sowie einen knapp 170 Quadratmeter großen Saal. Der Entwurf sah für die unterschiedlichen Nutzungen jeweils eigene Gebäudeteile vor, die sich in Größe, Struktur und Materialien deutlich voneinander unterscheiden. Das Theater wurde in die Mitte des Ensembles platziert und spielt sozusagen die architektonische Hauptrolle. Die schiere Masse dieses zentralen Gebäudes wird durch die Verwendung von braunem Beton betont, dessen erschlagende Präsenz aber durch den Einsatz leichter Metallverkleidungen abgemildert wird. Sie verbergen auch die Haustechnik. Das Innere gibt sich verspielt und heischt mit kräftigen Farben um die Aufmerksamkeit der Besucher. Eine dramatische Inszenierung bietet der Theatersaal: Der Raum ist komplett in einem leuchtenden Zinnoberton gehalten. Auch die nachgeordneten Kinosäle sind mit einem Blick für überraschende visuelle Effekte gestaltet. Obwohl sich die verschiedenen Nutzungen einen relativ kleinen Platz teilen müssen, wirkt alles klar und großzügig. Bunte, transluzente Brüstungsfelder an Treppen und Galerieetagen sowie eine zur Stadt hin verglaste Front öffnen das Gebäude auf eine splendide Weise und verbinden die Kunst mit dem Leben in der Stadt.

The new construction of a cultural centre was part of a comprehensive restructuring and modernisation of the town centre of Saint-Louis, a small town on the French-Swiss border near Basle. Alongside a multiplex cinema, the building includes a theatre and a hall of about 170 square metres in area. The design planned for the individual building sections for various utilisations, clearly different from each other in size, structure and materials. The theatre was placed in the middle of the ensemble and plays the main role, architectonically speaking. The sheer mass of this central building is emphasised by the use of brown concrete, the overwhelming presence of which is toned down by the light metal panelling. This also hides the mechanical services. The interior has a playful atmosphere and clamours for the visitor's attention with powerful colours. The theatre hall offers a dramatic scene: the entire room is in a luminous cinnabar. The subordinate cinema halls are also designed with surprising visual effects. Although the various utilisations must share a relatively small area, everything has a clear and spacious effect. Colourful, translucent balustrades on stairs and balcony storeys, as well as a glazed front towards the town, open up the building in a splendid way, combining art with the life of the town.

Oben In allen Schattierungen: Die Farbe Lila [*Above* In all shades: The colour purple
Rechts Cafeteria im Foyer [*Right* Cafeteria in the foyer

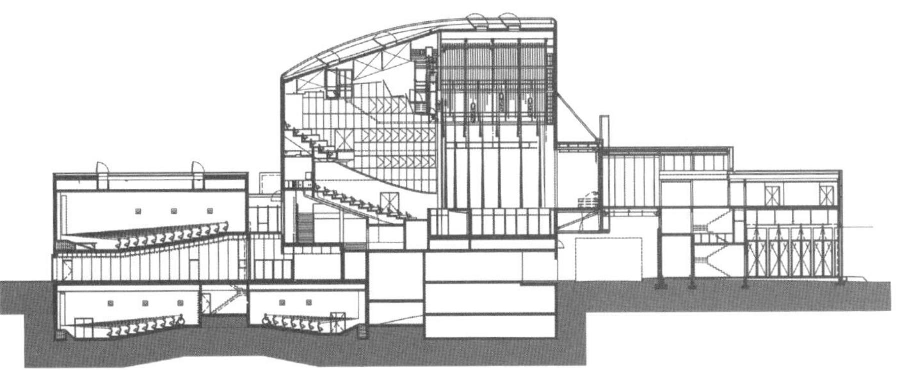

Unten Cineastenhimmel: Der große Kinosaal [*Below* Cineaste heaven: the large cinema hall

Oben Im Rausch der Farben: Theater- und Kinosaal [*Above* Ecstasy of colours: theatre and cinema hall

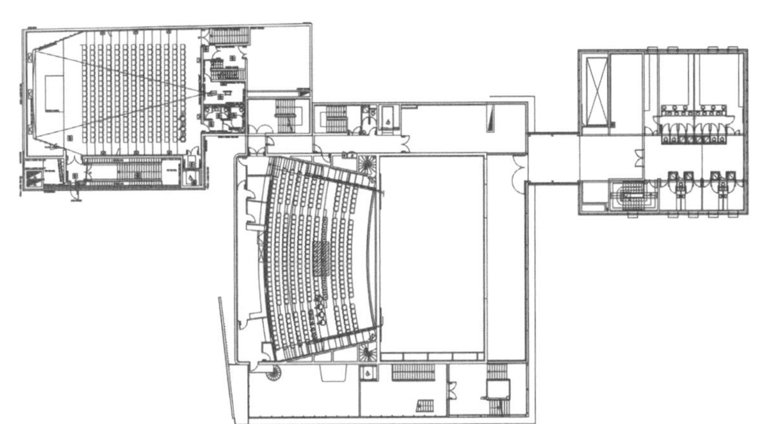

Maxim Gorki Theatre [Rouen [France [2004

Architects Jakob + MacFarlane [*Photographer* Jean-Marie Monthiers

Bei diesem Projekt ging es darum, ein bestehendes Theatergebäude mit einem neuen Zuschauerraum zu versehen und ganz nebenbei zwei prinzipielle Probleme des Altbaus zu lösen: teilweise unzureichende Sichtverhältnisse sowie schlechte Akustik. Die Spielstätte selbst besteht aus einzelnen Altbauten, die Anfang des 20. Jahrhunderts für die Errichtung eines Lichtspielhauses zusammengelegt wurden. Seit 1970 dient das Gebäude als Theater. Die kleinteilige historische Substanz sollte bei den Umbaumaßnahmen geschont werden. Doch im Hinblick auf eine Verbesserung der Gesamtsituation war es notwendig, ein neues Innenleben zu installieren. Es wurde ein lamellenartiges Gebilde aus Holz entwickelt, dessen Stufung die in ihrer Steigung optimierten Zuschauerränge antizipiert und im Scheitelbereich die akustischen und bühnentechnischen Einbauten integriert. Der so entstandene Raum wirkt wie eine dreidimensional erfahrbare Skulptur; die Farbe Rot ist eine Reminiszenz sowohl an die einst kommunistisch geprägte Stadt als auch eine ironische Erinnerung an die mit karminrotem Samt ausgekleideten Theaterräume der Belle Époque.

The aim of this project was to provide an already existing theatre with a new auditorium whilst, incidentally, solving two principal problems of the old building at the same time: insufficient visibility in places as well as poor acoustics. The theatre itself consists of individual old buildings which were put together for the construction of a cinema during the early twentieth century. The building has been a theatre since 1970. The small details of the historical substance were meant to be protected and preserved during the renovation. It was nonetheless necessary, with regard to improving the overall situation, to provide a new inner vitality. A rib-like structure was developed out of wood, anticipating the optimised audience-terraces in its ascent and integrating the acoustical and stage-technical installations into the area of focus. One experiences the resulting space as a three-dimensional sculpture; the colour red is reminiscent of the once communist-influenced city and also an ironical reminder of the theatrical rooms of the Belle Époque with their carmine-red silk lining.

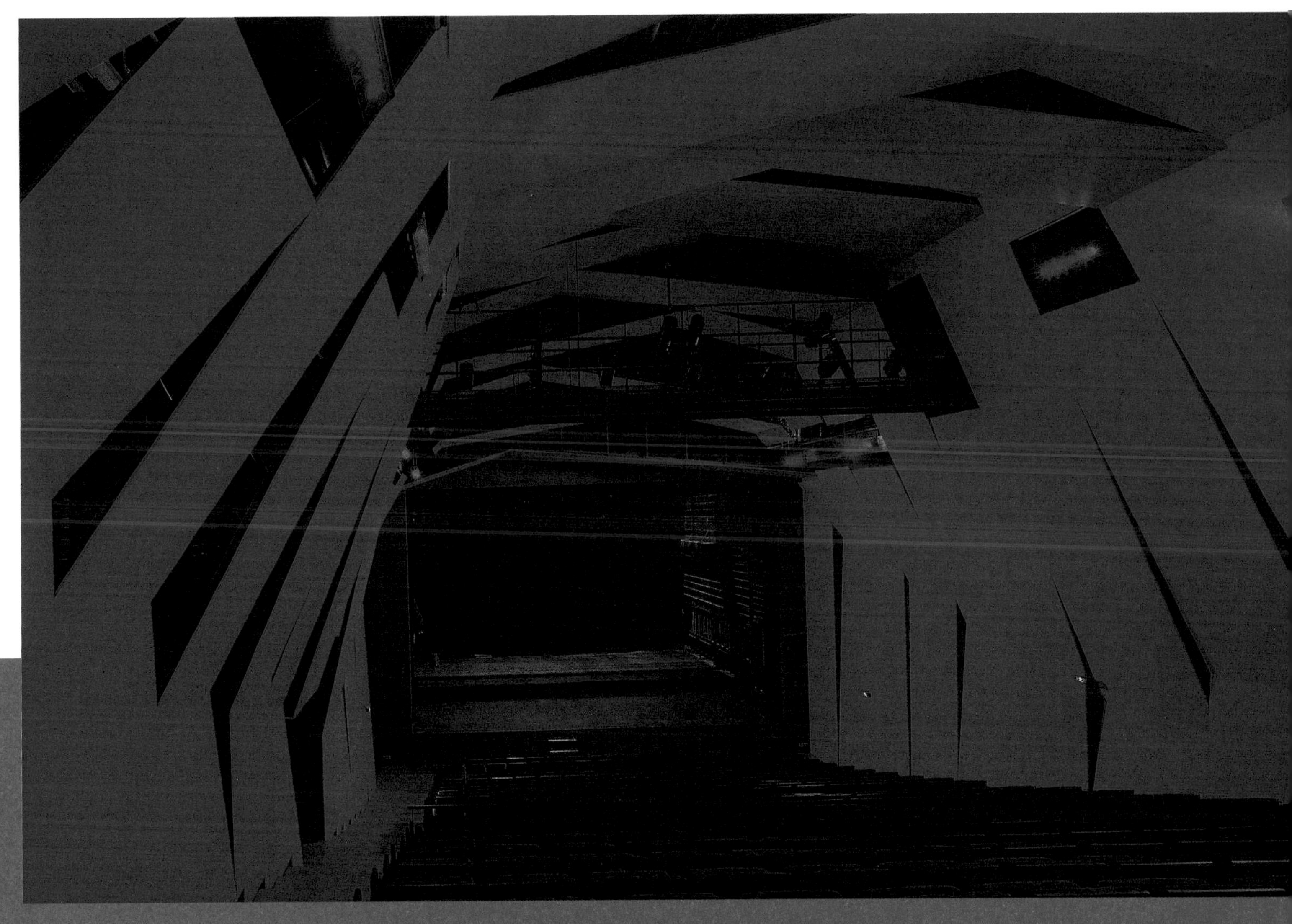

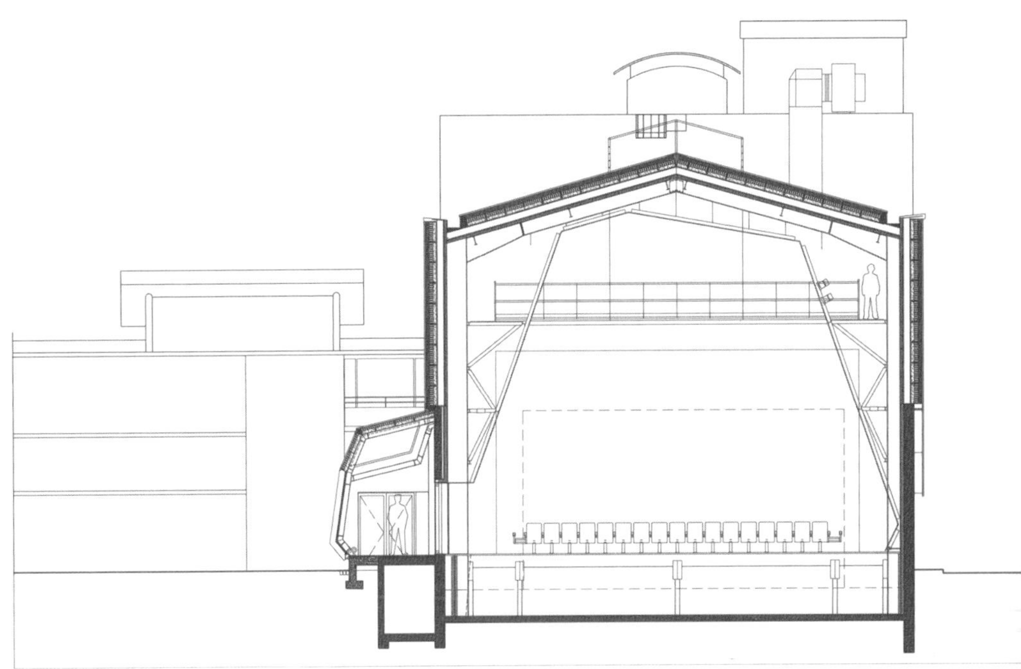

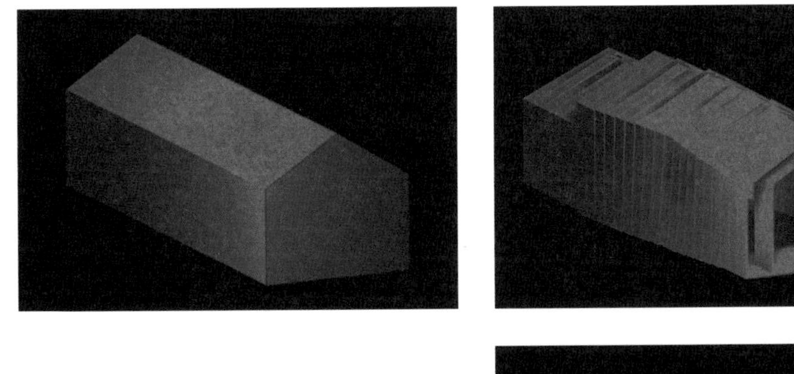

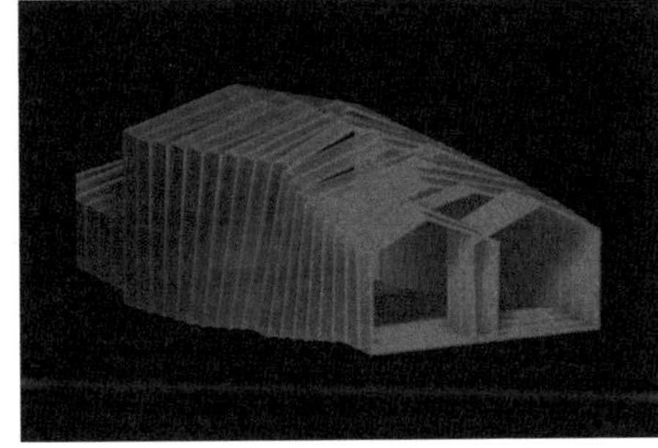

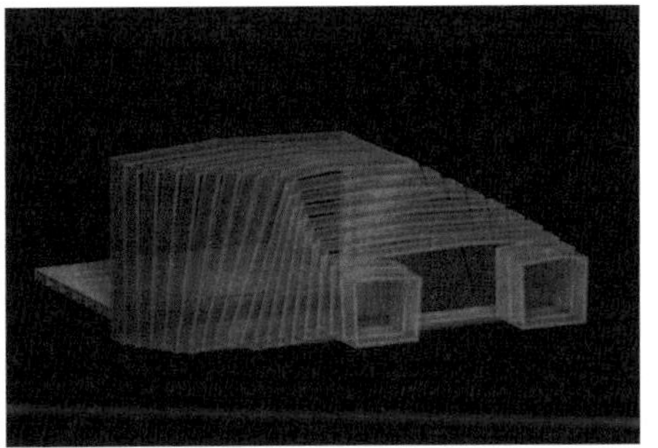

Links Rot gibt den Ton an im Theatersaal [*Left* Red sets the tone in the theatre hall [*Oben* Schnitt und virtuelles Modell [*Above* Section and virtual model

»Paris under Glass« Exhibition [Paris [France [1997

Architect Jacques Ferrier [*Photographers* Georges Fessy, Gaston Bergeret

An sich ist eine Architekturausstellung ein Paradox: Zu sehen sind ja immer nur Modelle des eigentlichen Exponats. So gesehen stellt der Pavillon de l'Arsenal quasi das Architektonische an der Ausstellung dar, und genau aus diesem Grund wird diese Struktur als optische Erscheinung auch zu einem Teil des Gezeigten. Über einen großen Spiegel wird das Gehäuse in die Leere über der Ausstellungsfläche projiziert. In dieser Ausstellung geht es um die Optik und Haptik des Transparenten: Glas. Die gläserne Stadt, also die Kristallpaläste von Passagen, Bahnhöfen und Kaufhäusern, wird ebenso abgehandelt wie die Geschichte des Fensters, der Mythos des Durchsichtigen, aber auch die verschiedenen Erscheinungsformen von Glas im Wandel der Zeiten und Moden. Daher setzt das Ausstellungsdesign konsequent auf transluzentes Industrieglas, das die transparenten und stofflichen Qualitäten des Materials erfahrbar macht. Es ist nicht völlig durchsichtig, doch man sieht Silhouetten, Farben, Bewegungen. Das Wechselspiel zwischen Reflexen, Grenzen, Vexierbildern und einer sich spiegelnden Architektur wird hier auf denkbar leichte Art und Weise inszeniert: ein Spiegelkabinett der Metropole.

An architecture exhibition is itself a paradox: one can only view models of the actual exhibits. Viewed in this way, the Pavillon de l'Arsenal represents the actual architectonic aspects of the exhibition; just for this reason, this structure as a visual appearance also becomes a part of what is being shown. The body is projected over a large mirror into the emptiness above the exhibition surface. The visual and haptic quality of transparency is the point of this exhibition. The glass city, the crystal palaces of passages, railway stations and department stores are treated just as are the history of the window, the myth of transparency, but also the different manifestations of glass over the ages and changing fashions. This is why the exhibition design consistently emphasises translucent industrial glass, enabling the viewer to experience the transparent and material qualities of the material. It is not completely transparent, but one sees silhouettes, colours and movements. The interplay between reflexes, boundaries, picture-puzzles and an architecture mirroring itself is staged here in a very light manner indeed: a mirror-cabinet of the metropolis.

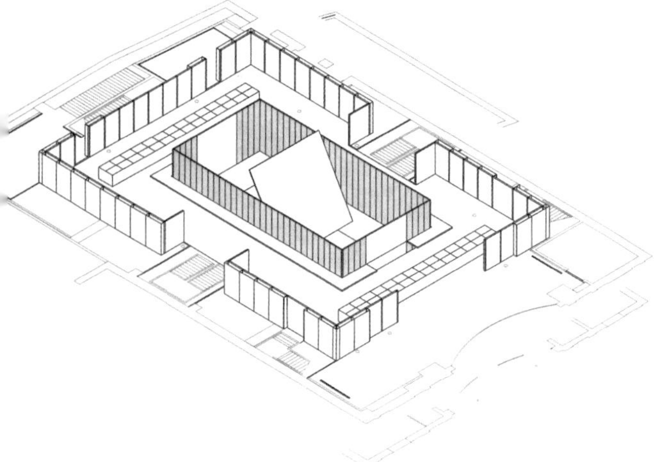

Links/Unten Im Glashaus: Rundgang durch die Ausstellung [*Left/Below* In the glasshouse: round tour through the exhibition

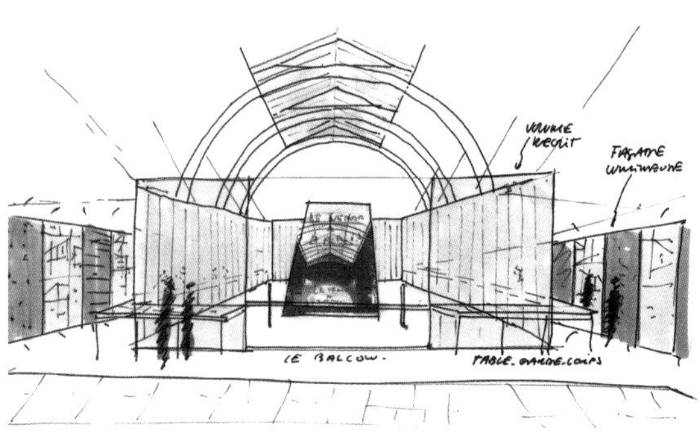

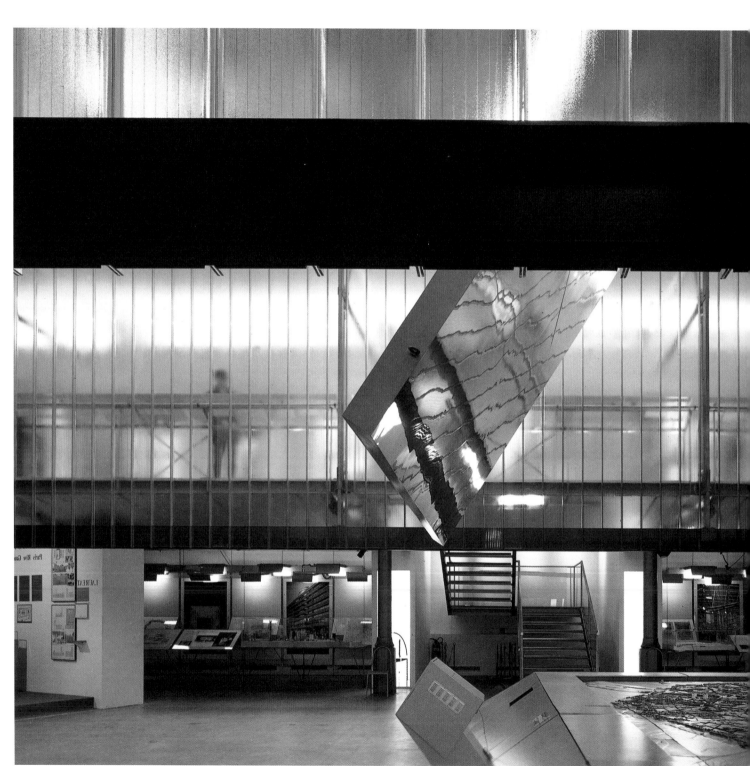

Oben Transluzente Glasfronten prägen den zentralen Raum [*Above* Translucent glass fronts mark the central room

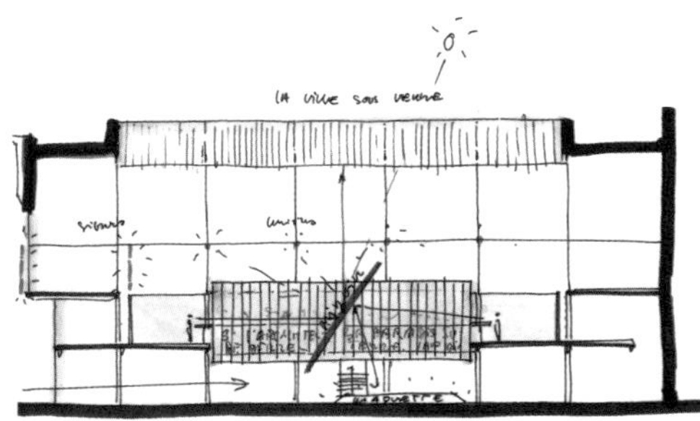

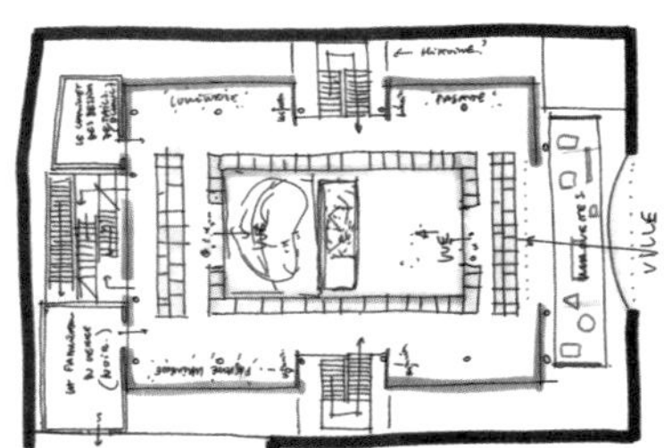

Library and Mediatheque [Raincy [France [2004

Architects Ameller & Dubois et Associés [*Photographer* Luc Boegly

Der Neubau einer modernen Multimediathek in der Stadt Raincy entstand als Erweiterung einer in einem großzügigen Park befindlichen historischen Villa. Es galt, die zahlreichen Ansprüche an ein zeitgemäßes, öffentliches Gebäude mit den Anforderungen des Denkmalschutzes zu verbinden. Die Villa wurde bereits vor der Errichtung des Annexbaus als städtische Bibliothek genutzt. Die Erweiterung ging mit einer umfassenden Neuorganisation des gesamten Hauses einher. Der Empfang ist nun in einer großzügig verglasten Veranda im Altbau platziert und führt direkt zu den Nutzer- und Leseräumen, die jetzt in dem neuen, geschwungenen Glaskorpus untergebracht sind. Die historischen Villenräume dienen nur noch Verwaltungszwecken. Die öffentlich zugänglichen Bereiche sind klar strukturiert und erschließen sich auf leichte, intuitive Weise. Der Kühle des transparenten Neubaus mit seiner gläsernen Haut und den plastisch ausgebildeten, tragenden Strukturen wurden gestalterische Kontrapunkte entgegengesetzt: Warme, freundliche Pastellfarben und vertraute Formen wie die der orangefarbenen Leselämpchen auf den Tischen sowie massives Mobiliar verleihen der Atmosphäre die nötige Ruhe.

The new construction of a modern multi-mediatheque in the city of Raincy originated as an extension of a historical villa situated in a spacious park. The intention was to combine the numerous requirements of a contemporary public building with those of monument protection. The villa was already being used as the city library before the construction of the annex. The extension went hand in hand with a comprehensive restructuring of the entire building. The reception is now located on a spacious, glazed veranda in the original part of the building and leads to the rooms for the users and readers, now in the new, curved glass corpus. The historical villa rooms now only serve administrative purposes. The areas accessible to the public are clearly structured and connected in light, intuitive ways. Contrasts have been placed in counterpoint to the coolness of the transparent new building with its glazed surface and the plastically formed supporting structures: warm, friendly pastel colours, familiar forms such as the little orange-coloured reading lamps on the tables as well as the massive furniture create the necessary calm atmosphere.

Links/Oben Entlang der sanft geschwungenen Fensterfront sind die Leseplätze gruppiert [*Left/Above* The reading places are grouped along the gently curved window front

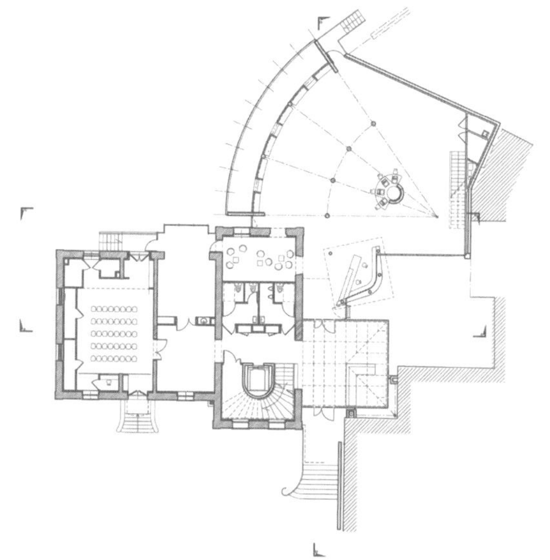

des dessinées

Unten Harmonisches Ganzes: Historische Villa mit modernem Anbau [Empfangsbereich [*Below* Perfect harmony: Historical villa wih modern annex [Reception area

SM´s Museum [´s-Hertogenbosch [The Netherlands [2005

Architect Matali Crasset [*Photographer* SM´s ´s-Hertogenbosch

Für dieses Museum für zeitgenössische Kunst und Design wurde eine alte Fabrikanlage revitalisiert, deren offene, undefinierte Raumfolge als eine Art Matrix für die neue Innengestaltung diente. Das schiere Ausmaß der Fläche erforderte zunächst ein integratives Element, mit dem nicht nur ein Zusammenhang zwischen den einzelnen Bereichen hergestellt wird, sondern das auch eine gewisse Ordnung und Orientierung schafft. So sind alle Räume über eine pistaziengrüne Schneise miteinander verbunden, die wie eine Hauptschlagader das gesamte Gebäude durchzieht und mit ihren feinen Verästelungen auch in die entlegeneren Winkel reicht. Je nachdem dienen ihre Ausläufer als Bibliothek, Restaurant, Verkaufsbereich oder Garderobe. Alle öffentlich zugänglichen Räume und Funktionen sind in der Farbe dieses Raumelements gehalten. Da das Gebäude relativ niedrige Deckenhöhen aufweist, wurde Wert auf eine lichte, sehr klare Einrichtung gelegt, die für Großzügigkeit und Offenheit sorgt. Meerfrische Farben wie kräftiges Türkis und Weiß, aber auch herzhafte Kontraste durch leuchtendes Magenta bringen Fröhlichkeit und Bewegung in das Museum. Aus dem Bekenntnis zum massenindustriellen Charme des Gebäudes und dem kühnen Einsatz postmodern interpretierter Retro-Optik ist eine zeitgeistige Architektur entstanden, die Schauwert hat.

An old factory building was revitalised for the museum, the open, undefined room-sequence of which served as a kind of matrix for the new interior design. The sheer size of the surfaces, first of all, required an integrative element with which not only a correlation between the individual areas would be made, but that would also produce a certain order and orientation. Thus all the rooms are connected to each other via a pistachio-green lane going through the entire building like a main artery, with its fine ramifications extending into the more out-of-the-way corners. Its outlets serve as library, restaurant, shopping area or cloakroom, depending on where you are. All publicly accessible rooms and functions are in the colour of this spatial element. Since the building has relatively low ceilings, much value has been placed upon very clear furnishing providing spaciousness and openness. Sea-fresh colours such as powerful turquoise and white, but also hearty contrasts through luminous magenta bring friendliness and movement into the museum. A kind of architecture reflecting the spirit of the times and with display value has arisen out of the belief in the building's mass-industrial charm and the courageous use of post-modern interpreted retro-optics.

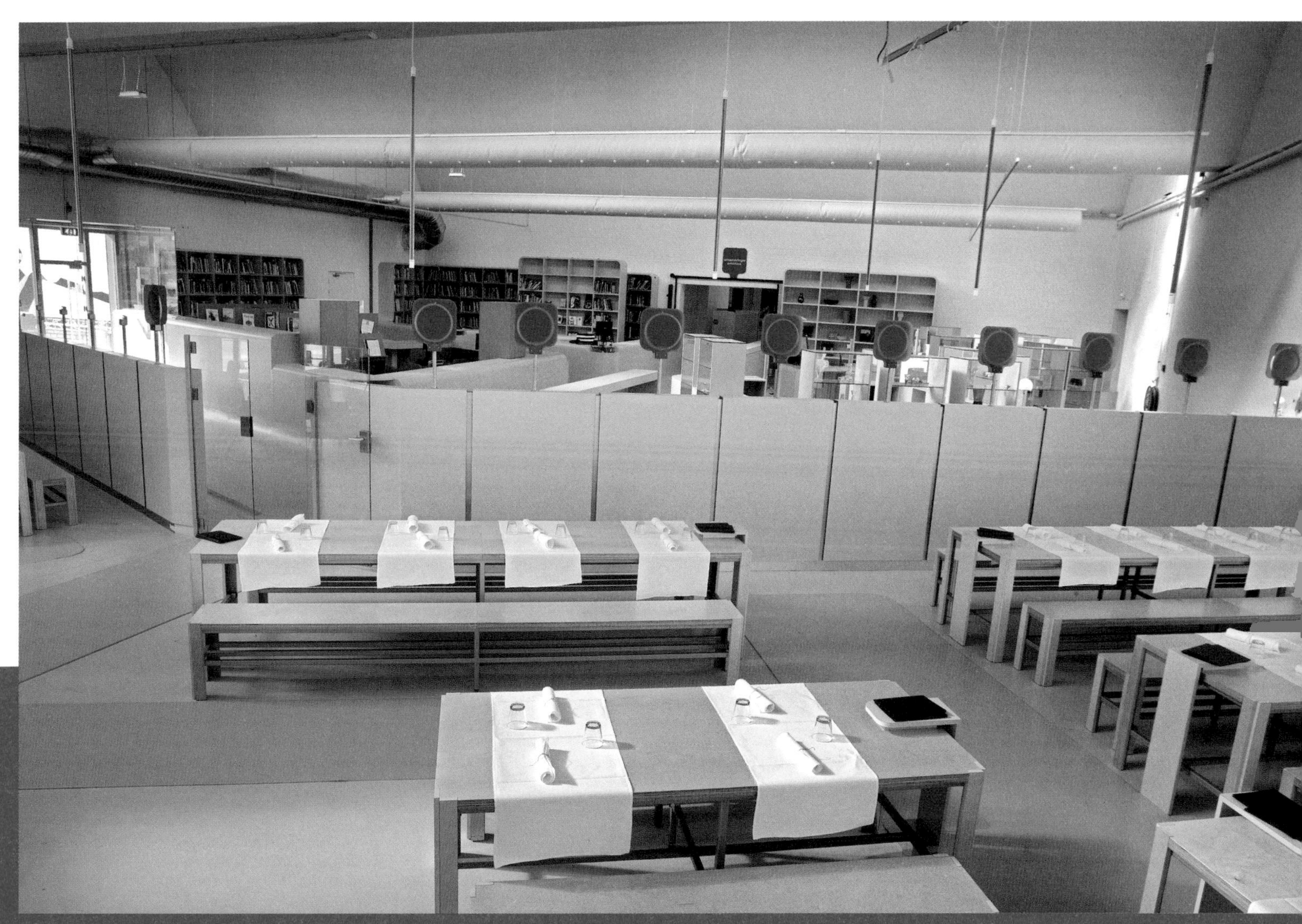

Links Auditorium [*Left* Auditorium [*Unten/Rechts* Eingangsbereich mit Bibliothek, Shop und Garderobe [*Below/Right* Reception area with library, shop and cloakroom

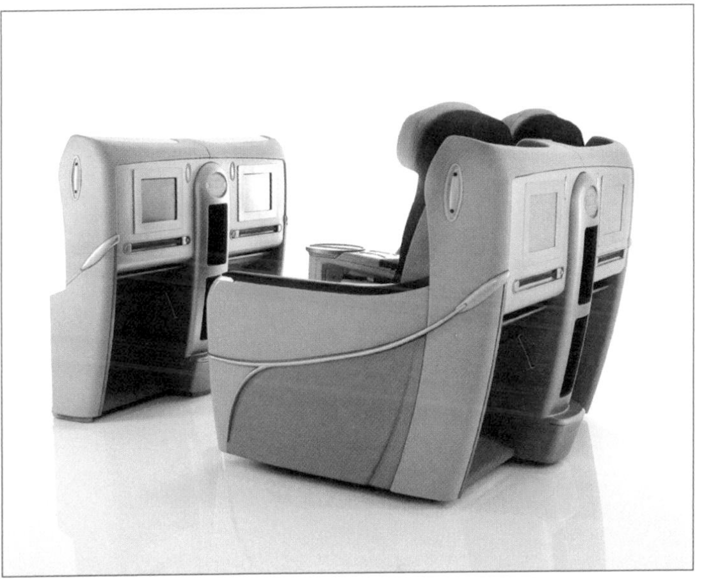

Oben/Links Auch das Mobiliar an Bord wurde von EGA entworfen; hier: Sessel der First Class
Above/Left The furniture on board was also designed by EGA; here: easy-chairs in the First Class area

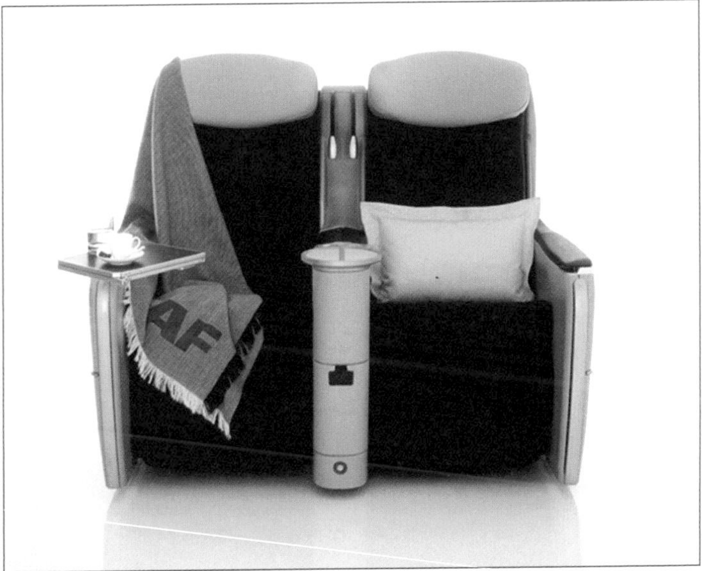

CLAY Fitness Center [New York [USA [2002

Architects Studios Architecture [*Photographers* Eric Laignel, Doug Fogelsow

Weil im verwöhnten Manhattan nichts härter bestraft wird als Langeweile, reicht für die Eröffnung eines neuen Fitnessstudios nicht nur geschäftlicher Wagemut. Eine außeralltägliche Idee ist unverzichtbar. Das dachten sich auch die Betreiber eines Wellness- und Sportzentrums am Union Square. Die vormals düstere zweite Etage eines Geschäftshauses aus den Dreißigerjahren wurde zu einem modernen, hellen Raum umgestaltet, in dem die landläufigen Vorstellungen von Ertüchtigungshallen mit Eleganz und Chic konfrontiert werden. Hier riecht es am Eingang nicht nach Schweiß und Seife, sondern nach dem harzigen Duft eines offenen Kaminfeuers, frischen Blumen und guten Drinks. Die eigens entworfenen Einbauten sind in einem sahnigen Weiß gehalten, für vornehme Akzente sorgen Kanten und Abschlüsse aus dunkel gebeizten Hölzern. Klare, geometrische Linien und gläserne Wände lassen eine offene, großzügige Atmosphäre entstehen, in der auch noch viel Platz für die selbstredend modernsten Sportgeräte ist. Die unterschiedlichen Bereiche sind klar voneinander getrennt, wenngleich die transparenten Raumabtrennungen immer für Durchblick sorgen. Von den Maschinen lässt sich ein weiter Blick auf die Stadt erleben. So ergibt sich das angenehme Wechselspiel zwischen Intimität und dem angenehmen Gefühl großstädtischer Anonymität wie von selbst. Für die entspannenden Momente nach den Übungen stehen den Kunden des Studios eine behagliche Lounge sowie ein Sonnendeck auf dem Dach zur Verfügung.

Since nothing is punished more harshly than boredom in pampered Manhattan, commercial daring alone is not enough for the opening of a new fitness studio – an extraordinary idea is indispensable. The operators of a wellness and sport centre on Union Square were also thinking along these lines. The formerly gloomy second storey of a commercial building from the 1930s was converted into a modern, bright space in which the commonly held ideas of physical training halls are confronted with elegance and chic. It doesn't smell like sweat and soap by the entrance here, but instead like the resinous aroma of a fireplace, fresh flowers and good drinks. The self-designed installations are in a creamy white, with borders and edges of dark, stained wood adding a noble touch. Clear, geometrical lines and glass walls provide an open, spacious atmosphere in which there is also plenty of space for the self-evidently most modern sport appliances. The various areas are clearly separated from each other, even if the transparent room-dividers provide a view. One can experience a wider view onto the city from the machines. The agreeable interplay between intimacy and the pleasant feeling of large-city anonymity results automatically. The clients of the studio have a comfortable lounge and a sun deck on the roof at their disposal for the relaxing moments following the exercise.

Oben Klarheit und Eleganz: Das Foyer [*Above* Clarity and elegance: the foyer

Oben Der Sanitärbereich . *Above* The sanitary area

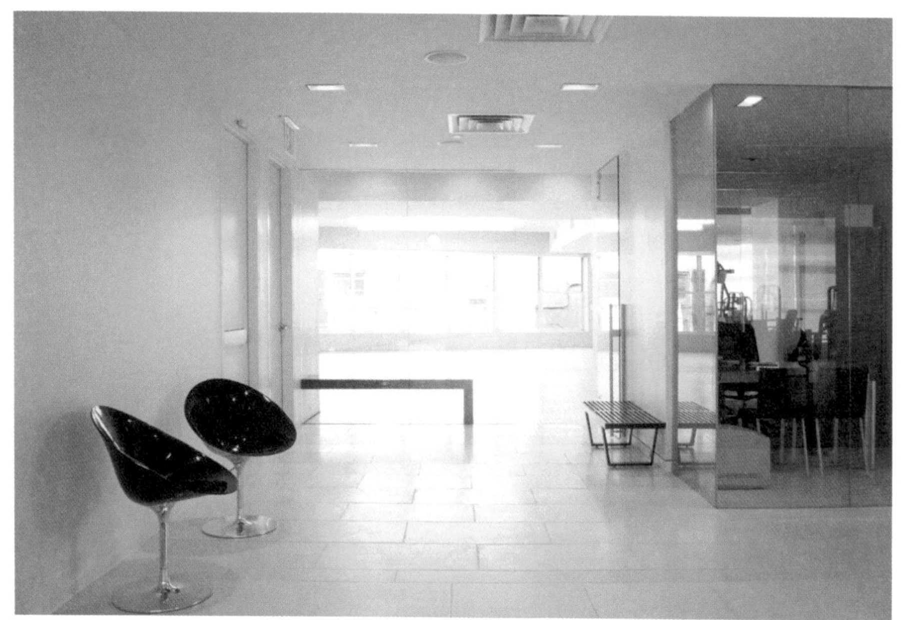

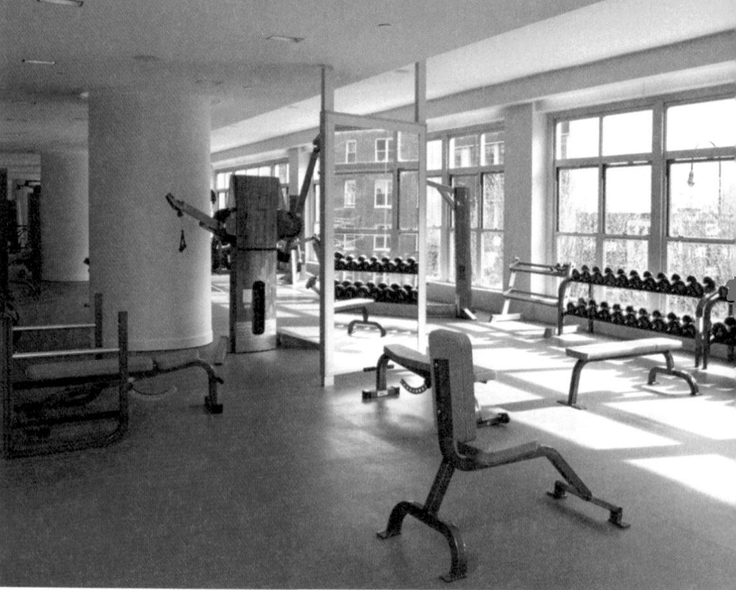

Oben Zimmer mit Aussicht: Der Trainingsbereich
Above Room with a view: the training area

Oben Umkleideraum [*Above* Locker room

Paris Tourist Office [Paris [France [2004

Architects CBA – Christian Biecher et Associés [*Photographer* Luc Boegly

Wer sich Paris nach Art des Reisenden nähern will, geht am besten dahin, wo die Stadt ihrem Klischee wohl am nächsten kommt: zum Boulevard Haussmann. In einem großen Eckgebäude residiert hier auf zwei Etagen die Touristeninformation, die sich nach dem Ausbau der Räumlichkeiten als kongeniale Verbindung aus Belle-Époque-Architektur und modernem Design präsentiert. Das Haus selbst hat den für Paris typischen trapezförmigen Grundriss, dem auch die gesamte Innengestaltung huldigt. Genau genommen bildet diese geometrische Figur die Determinante des Entwurfs, ihr geschickter Einsatz streckt den Raum optisch und führt den Blick weit nach innen. Eine wichtige Rolle spielt das Licht. Viele kleine, bündig in die Decke eingelassene Strahler sorgen für diffuse, indirekte Beleuchtung, und durch die großen Verglasungen zur Straße hin gelingt Tageslicht von draußen bis tief in den Raum. Die Einbauten unterstützen diese Lichtregie. So sind die tragenden Wände und Säulen mit teils blickdichten weißen, teils hinterleuchteten Glasflächen verkleidet. Gleichwohl sind diese Elemente mehr als nur statische Notwendigkeiten: Sie bergen Bildschirme, Telefone und Displays für Broschüren. Eine sparsame Möblierung sorgt in diesem stark frequentierten Raum für Offenheit und Großzügigkeit. Auch von außen kann sich der moderne Akzent gegenüber der prächtigen historischen Architektur behaupten.

Whoever wishes to approach Paris like a traveller is best advised to go where the city comes closest to its own cliché – to Boulevard Haussmann. The Tourist Information resides here on two storeys in a large corner building, presenting itself as a congenial combination of Belle Époque architecture and modern design after the expansion of its rooms. The building itself has the typical Parisian trapezoid-shaped floor-plan, also embraced by the entire interior design. To be precise, this geometrical figure is the determining factor of the design; its skilful application visually stretches the room, leading the observer's view far towards the inside. Light plays an important role here. Many small spotlights economically built into the ceiling provide diffuse, indirect lighting, and daylight from outside penetrates deeply into the room through the large glass openings facing the street. The installations support this stage direction of light. The supporting walls and pillars are partially covered with opaque white, and partially with glass surfaces with light shining from behind. Nonetheless, these elements are more than simply static necessities: they contain screens, telephones and displays for brochures. A sparing use of furniture guarantees openness and spaciousness in this heavily frequented room. From the outside, too, this modern accent stands up well alongside the splendid historical architecture.

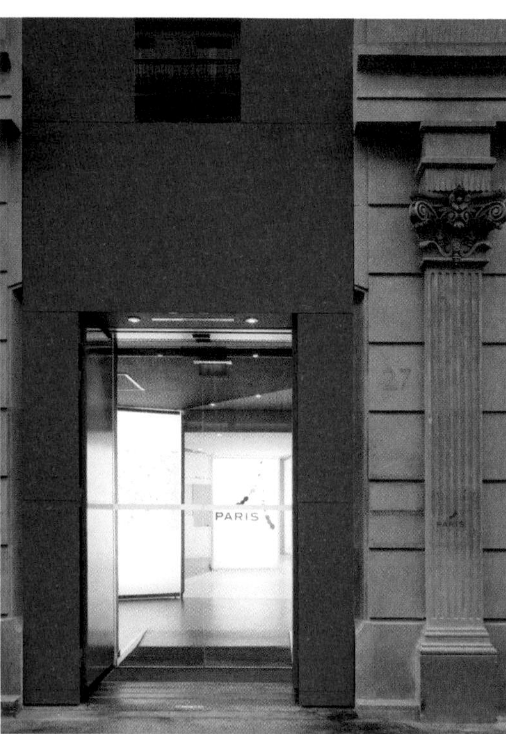

Oben/Rechts Alt neben Neu: Straßenfront [Klare, helle Farben dominieren das Interieur [*Above/Right* The old next to the new: street front [Clear, bright colours dominate the interior

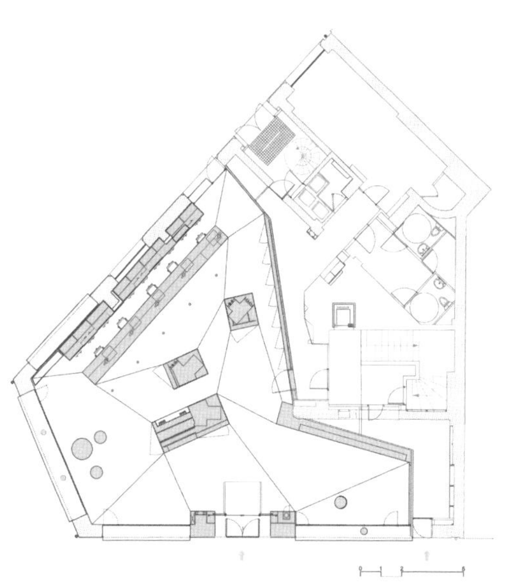

Oben/Rechts Sparsame Möblierung, klare Geometrie: Nichts verwirrt hier [*Above/Right* Sparse furnishing, clear geometry: no confusion here

CABARETS CABARETS
TITRES DE TRANSPORTS TRANSPORTATION PASSE

Bloomberg French Headquarters [Paris [France [2002

Architects Studios Architecture [*Photographer* Eric Laignel

Der französische Ableger eines weltweit operierenden Wirtschaftsnachrichtendienstes residiert in einem historischen, sechsgeschossigen Gebäude im Stadtzentrum. Freilich erforderte der Umbau ein wenig Courage, galt es doch, die patinierte Atmosphäre eines herrschaftlichen Stadtpalais behutsam zu renovieren und den Ansprüchen eines Medienunternehmens unterzuordnen. Die Gestaltung erfolgte mit großem Respekt vor solchen Preziosen wie Stuckdecken oder alten Fenstern, deren Charme die moderne Einrichtung adelt. Im Erdgeschoss befinden sich TV-Studios, ein Regieraum sowie ein Auditorium. Die erste Etage mit ihren öffentlichen Bereichen bildet das Herzstück des Gebäudes: Neben der Rezeption gibt es hier eine Cafeteria, die Fernsehredaktion sowie einen Schnittraum, eine Garderobe und einen Aufenthaltsraum. Das zweite Geschoss ist Konferenz- und Studioräumen vorbehalten. Die anderen Etagen beherbergen offene Büros und Besprechungsräume. In diesem Bereich verbreiten große Aquarien eine fast meditative Ruhe in der notorischen Hektik. Da die vorhandene Erschließung den Anforderungen nicht gerecht werden konnte, wurden zwei kühle, aus Granit und Stahl gefertigte Treppen eingebaut, die nun sämtliche Bereiche im ersten und zweiten Geschoss miteinander verbinden. Riesige, in Wände und Böden eingelassene Plasmabildschirme, große Hologramme sowie Monitore versichern dem Besucher auf Schritt und Tritt, dass er sich in der schnellen, flackernden Welt der weltumspannenden Kommunikation bewegt.

The French distributor of a worldwide operating economic news service resides in a historical, six-storey building in the centre of the city. The renovation required a bit of courage, of course, since the idea was to carefully renovate the patinated atmosphere of a magnificent urban palace and to subordinate the requirements of a media firm. The design took place with great respect for such fine details as stucco ceilings and old windows, the charm of which is ennobled by the modern facility. TV studios, a director's room and an auditorium are located on the ground floor. The heart of the building is formed by the first floor with its public areas: next to the reception there are a cafeteria, the television editors' office and a cutting room, a cloakroom and a lounge. The second storey is reserved for conference and studio rooms. The other storeys accommodate open offices and discussion rooms. Large aquariums in this area spread an almost meditative calmness in the notorious hectic. Since the former stairs could not meet the requirements, two cool, granite and steel stairways were built in; these now connect all the areas on the first and second floors. Giant plasma picture-screens built into floors and walls, large holograms and screens immediately assure the visitor that he/she is moving in the fast, flickering world of worldwide communication.

Oben/Rechts Schöne, neue Medienwelt: Futuristisch wirkt das Mobiliar, flackern die Monitore [*Above/Right* Brave new media world: the furniture has a futuristic effect and the monitors flicker

Oben/Rechts/Unten So sitzt man bei Bloomberg
Above/Right/Below This is how you sit at Bloomberg

LVMH Headquarters [Paris-Boulogne [France [2003

Architects Studios Architecture [*Photographer* Luc Boegly

Der größte Luxuskonzern der Welt, bekannt für edlen Champagner und teure Kosmetik, stand vor einer Reorganisation seiner Konzernzentrale. Beispielhaft für das moderne Selbstverständnis des Unternehmens sollte ausgerechnet das Verwaltungsgebäude den Wandel von strengen, hierarchischen Strukturen hin zu einer offenen, transparenten Arbeitsatmosphäre repräsentieren. Die neue Gestaltung zollt dieser Entwicklung auf sehr dezente Weise Tribut: mit großzügigen Räumlichkeiten und überschaubaren Strukturen. Große Glaswände lassen das Tageslicht bis tief in das Gebäudeinnere dringen. Sämtliche haustechnischen Funktionsbereiche, die Treppenhäuser und Fahrstühle sowie die Abstellräume sind in einem Trakt untergebracht, der sich als zentraler Riegel durch die Etagen zieht. Hier befinden sich auch Konferenz- und Besprechungsräume, Kopierstationen und Teeküchen. Wände und Böden sind in warmen, zurückhaltenden Naturfarben gehalten, das Mobiliar hingegen ist farbenfroh und bunt. Überall wurden Sitzgruppen, kleinere Besprechungseinheiten und Bereiche für spontane Unterredungen platziert, so dass die Arbeit nicht auf die Büros beschränkt ist, sondern im ganzen Haus stattfinden kann.

The world's largest luxury concern, famous for fine champagne and expensive cosmetics, was faced with a restructuring of its concern headquarters. The fact that the administration building was intended to represent the transformation from a strict, hierarchical structure to an open, transparent working atmosphere is exemplary for the modern firm's view of itself. The new design pays tribute to this development in a very subtle way with spacious rooms, clear structures and transparency. Large glass walls allow daylight to penetrate deeply into the interior of the building. All the mechanical service areas, stairwells, lifts and storage rooms are on one wing which goes through the storeys like a central bar. There are also conference and discussion rooms here, copying stations and tea-kitchen. Walls and floors are in warm, reserved natural colours; the furniture, on the other hand, is very colourful. Furniture ensembles, small discussion units and areas for spontaneous conversations are placed so that work is not limited to offices, but can take place anywhere in the building.

Oben Jederzeit möglich: Eine spontane Besprechung in den überall im Haus platzierten kleinen Sitzgruppen [*Above* Possible at any time: a spontaneous discussion in the small three-piece suites placed everywhere in the building

Oben Sitzbereich [*Above* Sitting area [*Unten* Grundriss [*Below* Floor plan

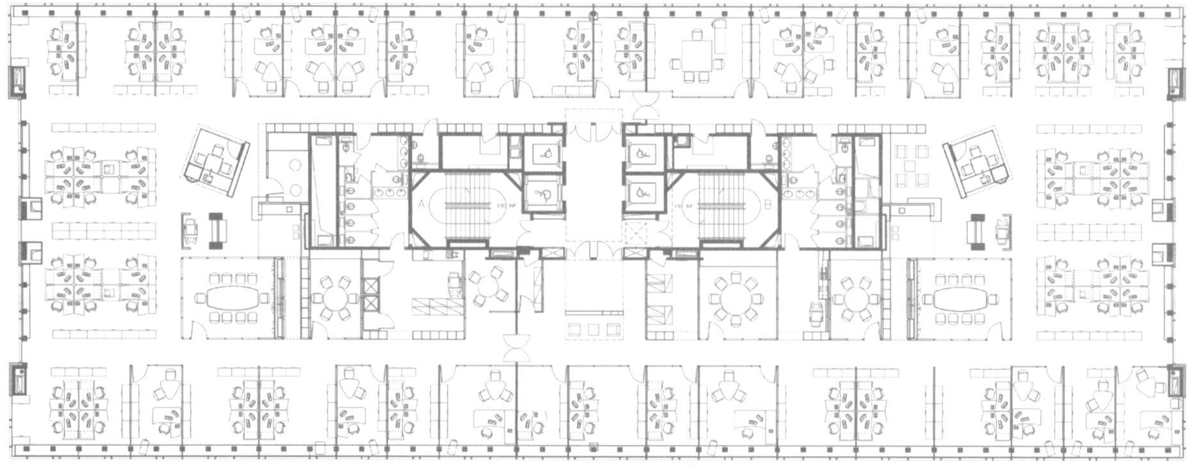

Oben Flur [*Above* Corridor [*Unten* Arbeitsbereiche [*Below* Working areas

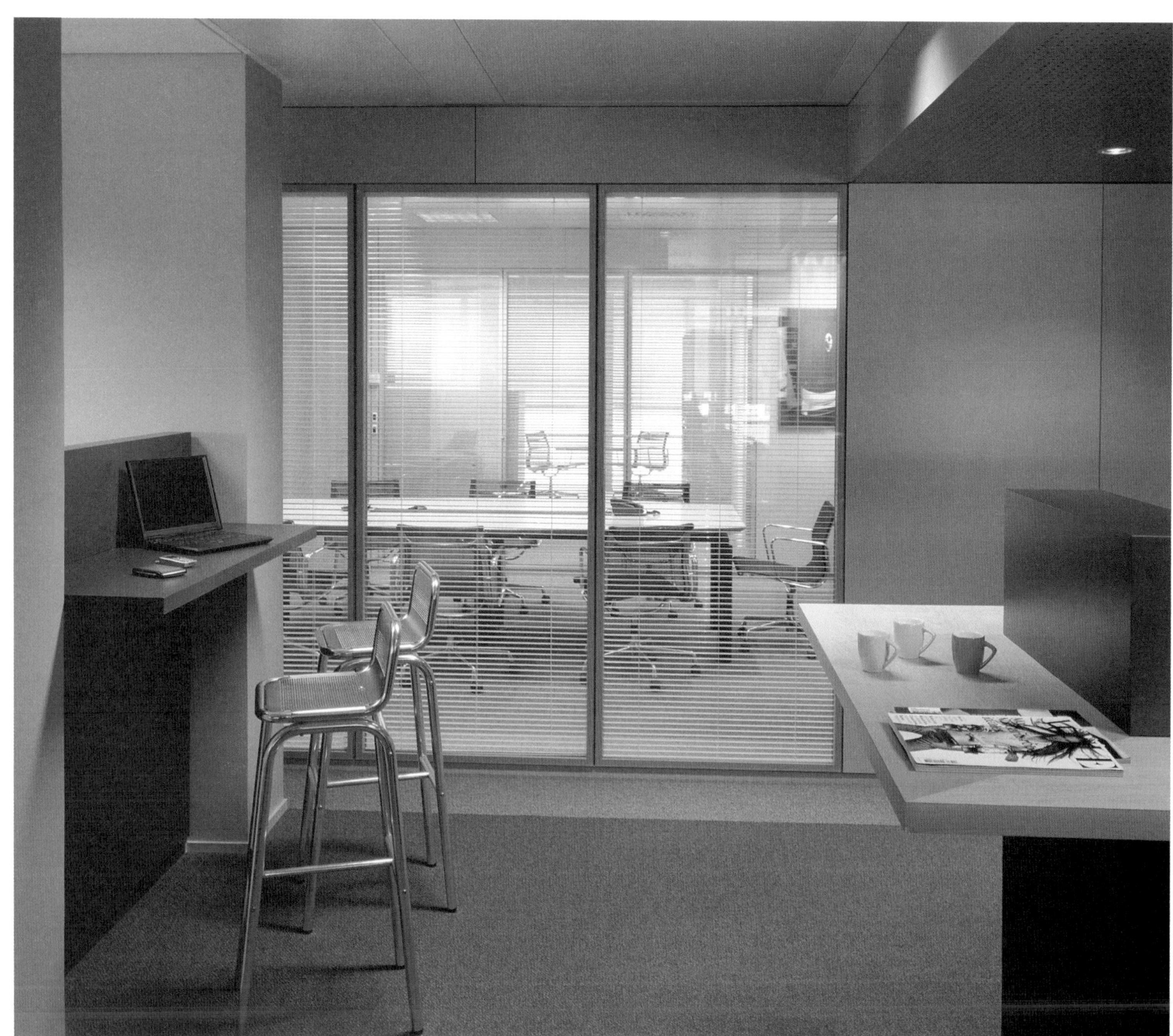

Oben/Rechts Gearbeitet werden kann praktisch überall, denn Glaswände und transluzente Raumteiler sorgen für die nötige Ruhe [*Above/Right* One can work practically everywhere because glass walls and translucent room dividers provide the necessary quiet

NSMD Bank [Paris [France [2003

Architects Arte Charpentier et Associés [*Photographer* Didier Boy de la Tour

Für die grundlegende Neugestaltung eines Bürohauses aus den Siebzigerjahren lobte eine private Geschäftsbank einen Architekturwettbewerb aus. Das in die Jahre gekommene Gebäude sollte seiner Lage im vornehmen 8. Arrondissement, einem traditionellen Geschäftsviertel, wieder gerecht werden und das Selbstverständnis einer erfolgreichen Bank verkörpern. Der siegreiche Entwurf hat den Baukörper in jeder Hinsicht geöffnet. Das Rückgrat bildet eine Achse, die sich durch das gesamte Gebäude zieht und nicht nur der Erschließung dient, sondern auch den Einfall von Tageslicht in alle Bereiche garantiert. Entlang dieser Achse wurden freie Treppen aus Holz und Metall platziert, die zusammen mit dem weißen Natursteinboden eine transparente, lichte Atmosphäre erzeugen. Die Akzente bleiben dezent: Lediglich im Bereich der Rezeption sowie an den Fahrstühlen fand warmes Holz Verwendung. Im Gegensatz zu der klaren, offenen Stimmung der öffentlichen Bereiche des Gebäudes vermitteln die Konferenz- und Besprechungsräume einen eher intimen, vertraulichen Eindruck. Der Boden hier ist mit einem dicken, schallschluckenden Teppich versehen, dessen kräftiges Rot sehr schön mit den teuer und fein verarbeiteten Tischen und Wandverkleidungen aus Holz harmoniert.

A private commerce bank held an architectural competition for the basically new design of a 1970s office building. It was hoped that the aging building would again do justice to its location in the noble 8th Arrondissement, a traditionally commercial quarter, and embody the self-image of a successful bank. The winning design opened up the body of the building in every respect. The backbone forms an axis continuing through the entire building, not only serving to connect things but also guaranteeing daylight in all areas. Free stairs of wood and metal were placed along the axis, creating a transparent, bright atmosphere together with the white natural-stone floor. The special touches remain subtle: warm wood is used only in the reception area and the lift. In contrast to the clear, open mood of the public areas of the building, the conference and discussion rooms communicate a more intimate, familiar impression. Here the floor is provided with a thick, sound-absorbing carpet, the powerful red colour of which beautifully harmonises with the expensive and finely developed tables and wall panelling.

Oben Hell und luftig: Das großzügige Foyer [*Above* Bright and airy: the expansive foyer [*Rechts* Dunkles Holz setzt warme Akzente [*Right* Dark wood sets warm accents

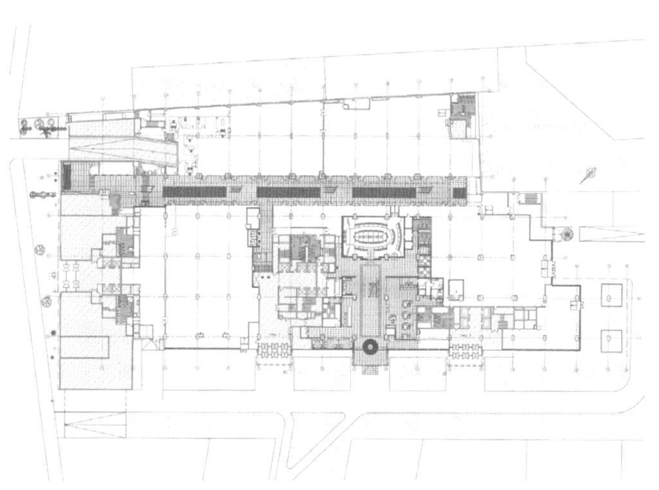

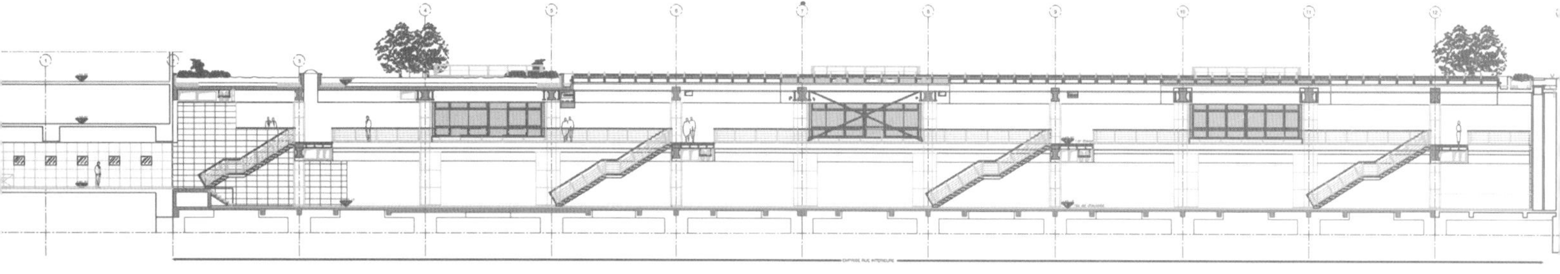

Links/Oben Besprechungsräume [Konferenzsaal [*Left/Above* Meeting rooms [Conference room

MTV Networks [New York [USA [2002

Architects Studios Architecture [*Photographer* Luc Boegly

Für eine neue Marketing-Abteilung ließ der größte Musiksender der Welt seine Zentrale am Times Square in Manhattan um eine ganze Etage erweitern und neu gestalten. Der Entwurf sah vor, eine atmosphärische Entsprechung der vielgestaltigen Programme des Senders zu schaffen: Licht, Farben und Materialien sollten die Räumlichkeiten in ein Schaufenster der globalen Popkultur verwandeln. Schon beim Verlassen des Fahrstuhls betritt der Besucher ein Reich, in dem das Imprägnierbad eines unberechenbaren Zeitgeistes noch jede Alltäglichkeit zur Ikone werden lässt. Großflächige, hinterleuchtete Aufnahmen von rauer, vereister Landschaft kollidieren mit der fabrikhaften Ungeschlachtheit der baulichen Strukturen und den glänzenden, kühlen Fluren, die teilweise in Farbe getaucht zu sein scheinen. Die schiere Größe der Fläche vermittelt Erhabenheit und Weite. Büros und Arbeitsbereiche wurden modern und nüchtern eingerichtet, die Farben sind lebendig, zum Teil überraschend und mit Mut zum Kontrast kombiniert. Es herrscht zweifellos eine sehr junge, frische Stimmung, die viel von der Betriebsamkeit eines Fernsehsenders hat und gut zur geschäftigen, rührigen Atmosphäre New Yorks passt. Doch dann gibt es auch ganz behagliche Sitzgruppen, die nicht mehr Lounge, aber auch nicht Business Class sein wollen. Hier lässt es sich aushalten. Vor allem mit der Aussicht auf den Mittelpunkt der Hauptstadt der Welt.

The world's largest broadcaster of music had its headquarters on Times Square in Manhattan expanded by an entire storey and newly designed for a new marketing department. The design was planned to create an atmosphere corresponding to the station's wide-ranging programme. Light, colours and materials were intended to transform the rooms into a display window of global pop-culture. Already when the visitor leaves the lift, he/she enters a realm in which the impregnating bath of an unpredictable spirit of the times transforms each banality into an icon. Spacious illuminated photos of rough, icy landscapes collide with the factory-like bulk of the building's structures and the shiny, cool corridors which at times seem to be dipped in colour. The sheer size of the surface communicates grandeur and space. Offices and workplaces have been furnished in a modern, no-nonsense way; the colours are lively, at times surprising and forming courageous contrasts. Without doubt a very youthful, fresh mood dominates, having a lot to do with the busy atmosphere of a television station and fitting in well with New York, the city that never sleeps. Then there are also very comfortable furniture ensembles, neither lounge nor business class. These are good places to relax, especially with a view onto the centre of the world's capital.

Oben/Rechts Club-Atmosphäre mit Aussicht [*Above/Right* Club atmosphere with a view

HOTELS

Ogilvy Advertising Agency [Paris [France [2005

Architects Atelier SoA Architectes [*Photographer* Marianne Rosenstiehl

Das alte Stadtpalais stammt aus der ersten Hälfte des 19. Jahrhunderts und wurde in den Dreißigerjahren des vergangenen Jahrhunderts um zwei Geschosse erweitert – und zwar von Le Corbusier. Nach einer umfassenden Modernisierung präsentiert sich der heterogene Komplex nun als höchst anregende Adresse, die sich das überall vorherrschende kräftige Rot – Markenzeichen der Agentur – als selbstbewusstes Wiedererkennungszeichen durchaus leisten kann.
Reste der spätbarocken Strukturen sind nur noch in den Räumen der ersten Etage erhalten – ihnen galt der konservatorische Ehrgeiz der Architekten, die großen Wert auf den Erhalt der ursprünglichen Pracht legten. Der repräsentative Mehrwert dieser Räume führte gar dazu, dass die Geschäftsführung, die normalerweise immer in den oberen Etagen residiert, diesen Bereich für sich reklamierte. Die Herausforderung bestand in der Schaffung eines internen, atmosphärischen Zusammenhangs zwischen den unterschiedlichen Räumen und Ebenen. Überall finden sich große, zusammenhängende Flächen und Einbauten aus gebürstetem Edelstahl und weißem Lack, die einen starken Kontrast zu dem signalartigen Zinnoberton bilden. Die Arbeitsplätze wurden in zentralen Bereichen konzentriert; Einzelrechnerstationen befinden sich in Alkoven. Glaseinlassungen in Decken versorgen auch das Innere des Gebäudes mit Tageslicht.

The old city palace was built during the first half of the 19th century and was expanded by two storeys during the 1930s – by Le Corbusier. The heterogeneous complex now presents itself as a highly stimulating address after a comprehensive modernisation; it can certainly show the every-present powerful colour red – trademark of the agency – as a confident sign of recognition.
Remains of the late baroque structures are only contained in the rooms of the first storey – the ambitious yet conservative architects greatly valued the preservation of the original splendour. The representative added value of these rooms led to the management claiming this area for itself, instead of taking up residence in the upper storeys as usual. The challenge was the creation of an internal, atmospheric correlation between the different rooms and levels. There are large, related surfaces and installations of brushed stainless steel and white varnish everywhere, forming a strong contrast to the signal-like cinnabar tone. The working areas have been concentrated into the central areas; individual calculating stations are found in alcoves. Glass openings in the roofs allow for plenty of daylight in the interior of the building.

Oben Signalroter Teppich, weiße Einbauten: Die Agentur setzt auf Kontraste [*Above* Signal-red carpet, white installations: the agency emphasises contrasts

Oben/Unten Details der Inneneinrichtung [Porträt und Signatur des legendären Gründers der Agentur, David Ogilvy [Sitzbereich [*Above/Below* Details of the interior installation [Portrait of the legendary founder of the agency, advertising guru David Ogilvy, as well as his signature [Sitting area

Oben Klares, geradliniges Design bestimmt die Atmosphäre in den Arbeitsbereichen [*Above* Clear, straight design in the working areas [*Rechts* Isometrie [*Right* Isometry

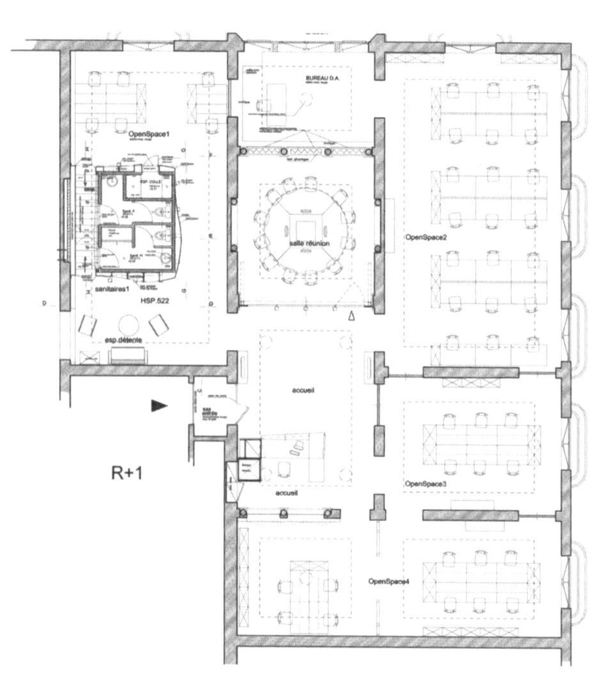
BUREAU D.A
OpenSpace1
salle réunion
OpenSpace2
sanitaires1
HSP 522
esp détente
accueil
OpenSpace3
accueil
OpenSpace4
R+1

Links/Rechts Noblesse oblige: Der Vorstand residiert in den historischen Räumen
Left/Right Noblesse oblige: the Board of Directors resides in the historical rooms

Oben/Rechts Modernes Design in historischem Ambiente [*Above/Right* Modern design in a historical atmosphere

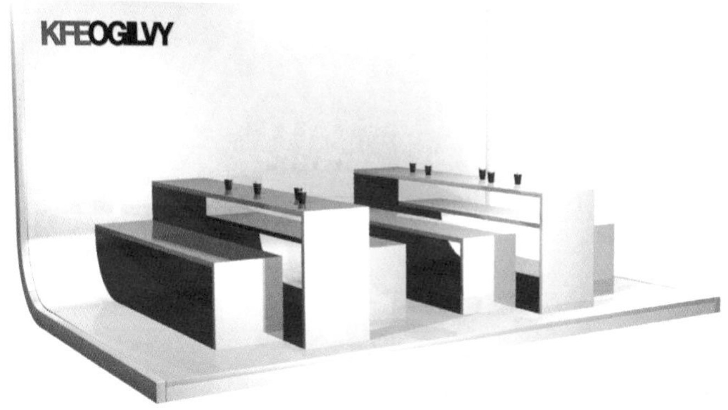
KFEOGILVY

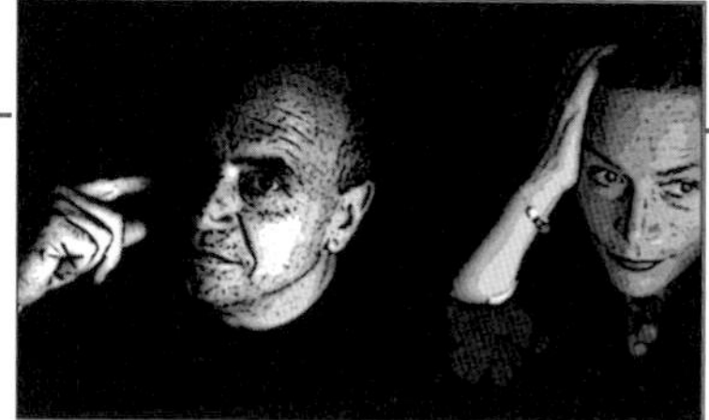

Armani Jeans [Milan [Italy [2004

Architects Massimiliano + Doriana Fuksas [*Photographer* Maurizio Marcato

Mit ihren glänzenden Oberflächen, den erratischen Lichtreflexen und überraschenden Ecken und Winkeln sieht die Boutique des bekannten italienischen Edeldesigners aus wie begehbarer Cyberspace – irgendwie galaktisch. Ein großes Ladengeschäft in Europas Modehauptstadt Mailand wurde für die sportlich-juvenile Linie des Couturiers zu einem irrwitzigen Parcours ausgebaut, der in seiner Weite und Großzügigkeit vor allem eines ist: luxuriös.

Um den präsentierten Waren einen großartigen Auftritt zu verschaffen, sollte die Architektur dezent in den Hintergrund treten und für die Kleider, Schuhe und Accessoires mit den ihr eigenen Mitteln einen wirkungsvollen Rahmen schaffen. Dafür beschränkten sich die Architekten auf den Einsatz hochglänzenden Kunststoffs. Mit diesem Material wurden die fixen Strukturen verkleidet; Ecken, Kanten und Makel verschwanden unter der gleißenden Hülle, die Vorzüge des Raums und vor allem der Waren wurden betont.

Im Prinzip taten die Architekten nichts anderers, als dem Laden ein schmeichelndes Kleid zu schneidern. Die Einrichtung wurde so flexibel gestaltet, dass die textilen Preziosen sich immer wieder neu und anders inszenieren lassen. Regale, Displays und Kleiderständer können flexibel positioniert werden, die unterschiedlichen Bereiche des Ladens gehen ineinander über. Licht und Farben lösen die Formen auf – alles fließt.

With its shining surfaces, erratic light reflexes and surprising nooks and crannies, the boutique of a famous Italian noble-designer looks like a cyberspace that one could walk on – somehow galactic. A large department store in Europe's fashion capital Milan was expanded into a riotous parcours for the fashion designer's sportive, youthful line. In its breadth and spaciousness, it is one thing above all: luxurious.

To allow for a magnificent display of the goods being presented, the architecture should subtly retreat into the background, creating its own effective space for the clothing, shoes and accessories with its own means. To achieve this, the design was limited to the use of high-gloss plastic. The fixed structures were covered with this material; corners, edges and flaws disappeared under this lustrous shell; the advantages of the rooms and especially the goods were emphasised. In principle, the architects did nothing but cut a flattering dress for the shop. The installation was designed so flexibly that the precious textiles could always be staged anew and differently. All shelves, displays and clothes racks can be flexibly positioned; the different areas of the shop blend into each other. Light and colour dissolve the forms: everything flows.

Links/Oben Planet Armani Jeans: Hier dreht sich alles um edles Denim [*Left/Above* Planet Armani Jeans: everything here is focused on noble denim

Oben Moderne Materialien unterstreichen das jugendliche Image des Modelabels [*Above* Modern materials emphasise the youthful image of the fashion label

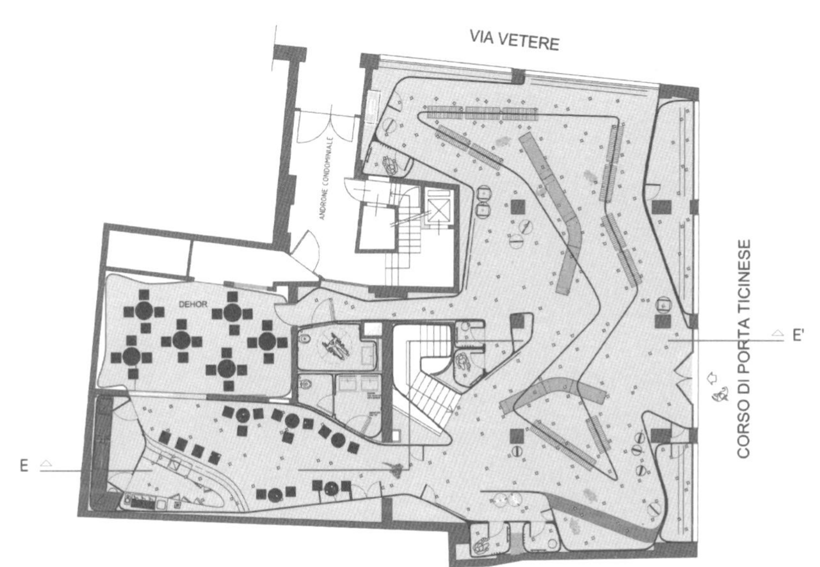
VIA VETERE
ANDRONE CONDOMINIALE
DEHOR
CORSO DI PORTA TICINESE
E
E'

BHV Annex [Paris [France [2004

Architect Matali Crasset [*Photographer* Patrick Gries

Man könnte die neue Abteilung im Untergeschoss eines großen französischen Einkaufszentrums wahrscheinlich als juveniles Lifestyle-Department bezeichnen, würde es nicht doch etwas mehr sein wollen als ein normaler Konsumtempel für Teenager. Das Kaufhaus wagte ein Experiment und öffnete seine Räume auch für die unspektakulären Alltagspraktiken Jugendlicher, in deren Leben nun einmal Schulen und Sportvereine eine ebenso große Rolle spielen wie Musik, Mode und Freizeit. Diese Aspekte wurden über ein neues räumliches Konzept integriert und gestalterisch auf höchst eigenwillige, ausgesprochen zeitgeistige Art übersetzt, die auch die Grenzen zwischen Konsum, Freizeit, Schule und Beruf verschwimmen lässt und ausschließlich auf die jugendliche Kundschaft zugeschnitten ist. Die gesamte Fläche wurde in vier größere thematische Abschnitte gegliedert, die immer mehr sein wollen als nur Verkaufsstände für Mode, Sport, Musik und Design. Im zentralen Bereich, der die Abteilung auch mit den anderen Etagen des Hauses verbindet, finden die Besucher vor allem Informationen, Ausstellungen und Aktionen von Institutionen, Kultur- und Kunstvereinen sowie Bildungseinrichtungen. Die gesamte Einrichtung gibt sich jugendlich, trendy und extrovertiert. Knallige Neonfarben, Kunststoffoberflächen und Einbauten, die man als witzig bezeichnen kann, verwandeln das Geschoss in eine futuristische Kulisse, deren Aufenthaltsqualitäten vor allem Jüngere zu schätzen wissen.

One could probably designate the new department in the basement of major French department store as a juvenile lifestyle department, if it did not strive to be something more than a normal consumer-temple for teenagers. The department store risked an experiment and opened up its rooms to the unspectacular everyday activities of young people as well. After all, schools and sport clubs play as important a role in their lives as music, fashion and leisure. These aspects were integrated into a new spatial concept and translated into a highly wilful, pronouncedly contemporary design located between the boundaries of consumerism, leisure, school and profession, and yet exclusively tailor-made to young customers. The entire surface was divided into four large thematic sections which always strive to be more than merely sales-stands for fashion, sport, music and design. In the central area, also connecting the department with the other storeys of the building, the visitor finds information, exhibitions and events presented by institutions, cultural and artistic associations as well as educational facilities. The entire installation presents itself as youthful, trendy and extroverted. Glaring neon colours, plastic surfaces and humorous installations transform the storey into futuristic scenery especially appreciated by young people as a place to spend some time.

SORTIE DE SECOURS

Oben Für die Jüngsten: Spielzone [*Above* For the youngest guests: play area [*Rechts* Mini-Shop für Lebensmittel [*Right* Mini-Shop for groceries

Links/Rechts Verschiedene Abteilungen mit Mode und Accessoires [»Café Yelo«
Left/Right Various departments with fashion and accessories [»Café Yelo«

café
yelo
menus pâtes
pâtes fraîches
pâtes farcies
menu mezzo
menu presto
fraîcheurs

Oben Im Café können die jungen Kunden lesen, essen oder einfach nur relaxen [*Above* Young customers can read, eat or just relax in the café

Daum Glassware [Paris [France [2001

Architects EGA – Eric Gizard et Associés [*Photographer* Christophe Fillioux

Eine fast anrührende Zerbrechlichkeit umgibt diesen Laden in der rührigen Pariser Innenstadt. Zart und durchscheinend wirkt es hier; die Ruhe hat etwas Fernöstliches. Es ist ein Fachgeschäft für Glaskunst. Damit die fragil-transparenten Artefakte zur Geltung kommen, musste die Einrichtung sehr zurückhaltend gestaltet werden. Weiß als vorherrschende Farbe lässt noch jedem Hauch von Farbe den Vortritt; das indirekte, helle Licht umfängt die gläsernen Dinge in den Vitrinen und Schaukästen mit einem nahezu überirdischen Schein. Die Vorsicht, mit der sich die Besucher durch die Räume bewegen, wird zu Andacht. Die Auslageflächen sind bündig in die Wand eingelassen und wirken durch die schmalen Metallrahmen wie Kunstwerke. Alle ausgestellten Waren stehen auf halbdurchscheinenden Glasborden, deren glänzende Oberflächen an ruhiges Wasser erinnern. Den Räumen ist etwas Traumhaftes eigen; eine Atmosphäre, die der rauen Wirklichkeit nicht standhalten muss.

The shop in the busy Parisian inner city is surrounded by an almost touching fragility. It makes a tender and translucent effect; the calmness has an almost Far Eastern quality. It is a specialist shop for glass art. The installation must hold itself back considerably for the fragile, transparent artefacts to show themselves to their best advantage. White is the dominant colour, allowing precedence to each trace of colour; the indirect, bright light surrounds the glass objects in the display windows and showcases with an extraterrestrial quality. The care with which the visitor moves through the rooms becomes devotional. The display surfaces are concisely built into the walls and their narrow metal frames give them the effect of works of art. All the exhibited goods stand on translucent glass boards, the shining surfaces of which are reminiscent of calm water. The rooms have something dreamlike about them: an atmosphere that does not have to resist hard reality.

Links Kunst aus Glas hinter Glas [*Left* Art made of glass behind glass [*Rechts* Nahezu überirdisch erscheinen die in den schlichten Vitrinen präsentierten Exponate [*Right* The examples presented in the simple display windows have an almost heavenly effect

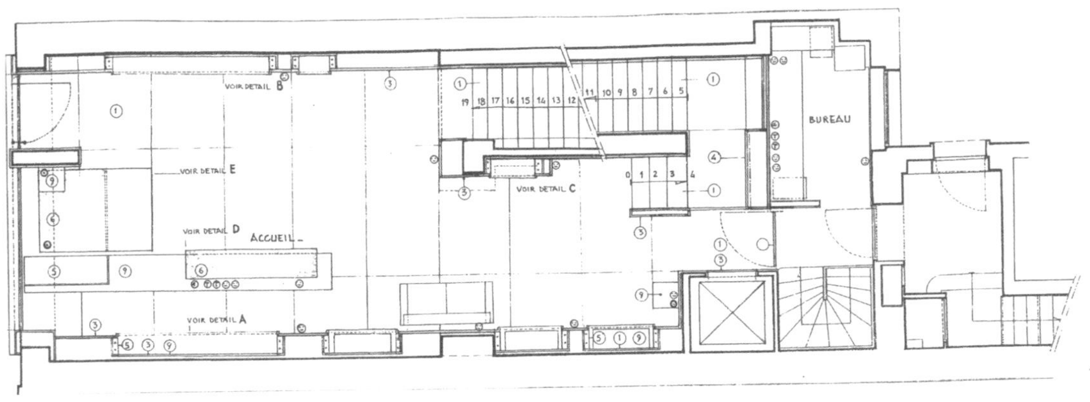
VOIR DETAIL B
BUREAU
VOIR DETAIL E
VOIR DETAIL C
VOIR DETAIL D
ACCUEIL
VOIR DETAIL A

Links/Unten Die filigranen Glaskunstwerke stehen im Vordergrund: Blick in den Verkaufsraum
Left/Below The filigree glass objects stand in the foreground: view into the sales room

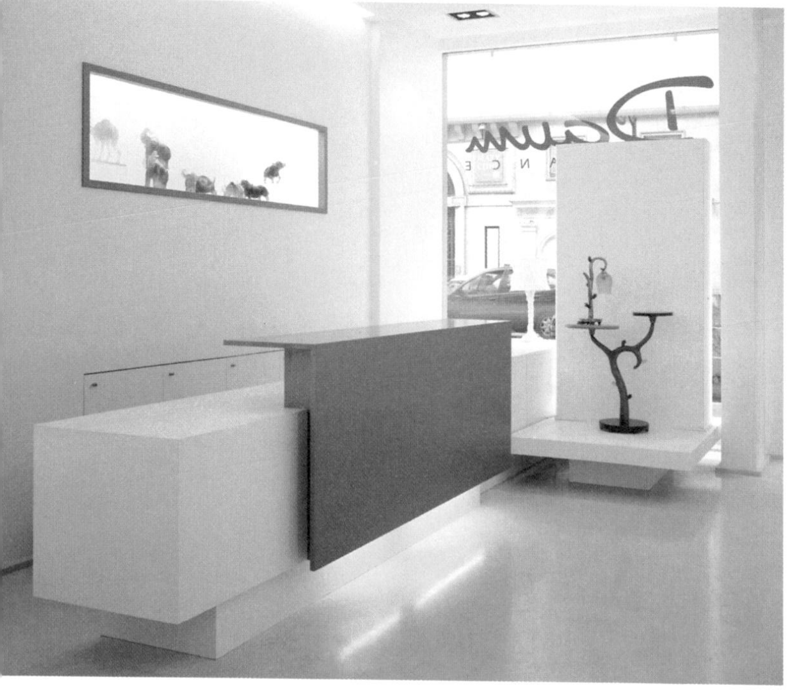

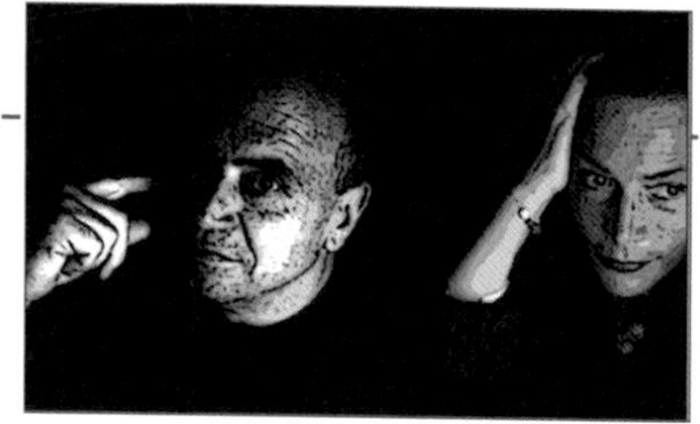

Emporio Armani [Hong Kong [China [2002

Architects Massimiliano + Doriana Fuksas [*Photographers* Ramon Prat, Maurizio Marcato

Als Leitmotiv bei der Gestaltung des Ladens diente den Architekten die Vorstellung eines Experimentierfeldes der Identitäten im Zeitalter der Globalisierung. Die Schlagwörter dieser Idee sind bekannt: Auflösung von Raum- und Zeitgrenzen, virtuelle Welten und Digitalisierung. Und es gibt wohl kaum einen besseren Botenstoff dieser neuen Ära als Mode. Und der Architektur kommt in diesem Zusammenhang einmal mehr die Funktion einer Hülle und Kulisse gleichermaßen zu. Hongkong ist ein dankbarer Ort für die Inszenierungen des weltumspannenden Luxuskonsums – die Stadt gilt als Chiffre für alles, was mit den Segnungen der Globalisierung verbunden wird. Diesem Futurismus huldigt auch der Entwurf. Jenseits aller Erwartungen an normale Geschäftsarchitektur thematisiert er die Bewegungen der Menschen im Raum, die Zufälligkeit ihrer Schritte. Die Materialien strotzen vor Technologie: gleißend, transparent, aseptisch. Der kühle, arrogante Raum selbst ist eine Durchdringung und Überlagerung von Ebenen; Spiegel, ein hochglänzender Epoxidharzboden sowie riesige Glasfronten verstärken mit erratischen Reflexionen diesen Effekt. Hier kauft man nicht einfach ein. Hier befindet man sich im Abflugterminal in Richtung Zukunft.

The idea of a field of experimentation of identities in the age of globalisation served the architects as a leitmotiv. The catchwords of this idea are well known: dissolution of spatial and temporal boundaries, virtual worlds and digitalisation. And there is hardly a better subject matter carrying the message of this new era than fashion. In this connection, architecture once again assumes the function of a shell as well as a stage. Hong Kong is a grateful place for the staging of global luxury consumerism – the city is considered a symbol for everything connected with the blessings of globalisation. The design also pays homage to this futurism. Going beyond all expectations of normal commercial architecture, it deals with the movement of people in the room, the chance occurrence of their steps. The materials are teeming with technology: shining, transparent, aseptic. The cool, arrogant room is itself a penetration and overlapping of levels: mirrors, a highly lustrous epoxide resin floor, along with giant glass fronts strengthen this effect with erratic reflections. One does not simply shop here. Here is where one finds oneself in the take-off terminal to tomorrow.

GIORGIO ARMANI

Rechts Im Vordergrund des Gestaltungskonzepts steht der leere Raum [Eingang Charter Road [*Right* The empty room stands in the foreground of the design concept [Entrance on Charter Road

Oben Exklusive Floristik gehört mittlerweile auch zum Portfolio des Modeimperiums [*Above* Exclusive floral art meanwhile also belongs to the portfolio of the fashion empire

FANDA
FANDA PERFUME CO.

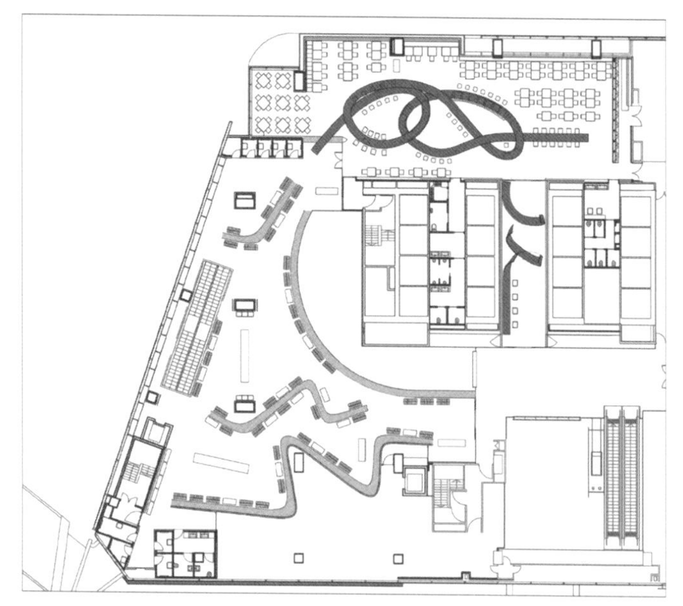

Links Grundriss, deutlich sichtbar das bestimmende und verbindende Element zwischen Verkaufsbereich und Restaurant: Ein Band aus rotem Fiberglas; Treppe aus Edelstahl und Plexiglas
Left Ground plan, clearly and visibly the decisive and connecting element between sales area and restaurant: a band out of red fibreglass; stairway of stainless steel and plexiglass
Unten Der Verkaufsraum, auch hier dominieren geschwungene Linien [*Below* Sales room: curved lines dominate here as well

Oben/Rechts Klarheit und Übersichtlichkeit prägen sowohl Innenräume als auch äußere Gestalt [*Above/Right* Clarity and a clear overview mark both the interior rooms and the outside design

EMPORIO ARMANI

Look.
YOU
RETRO

ESIGN
INSIDE HOLLYWOOD
DavidBailey
peter max
TUSCANY
WINETASTING
Wine

ALIENS
RANDOM ACCESS
Look.
YOU
RETRO

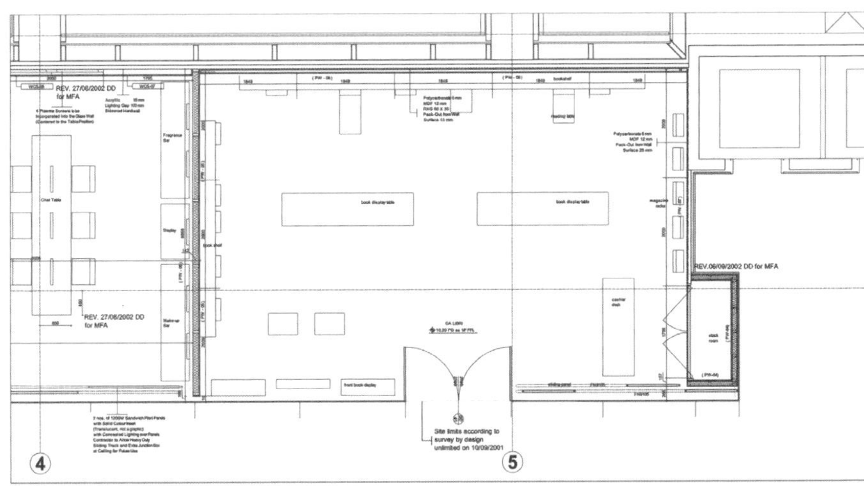

Links/Unten Armani Libri: Bildbände in exlusivem Interieur
Left/Below Armani Libri: illustrated books in the exclusive interior

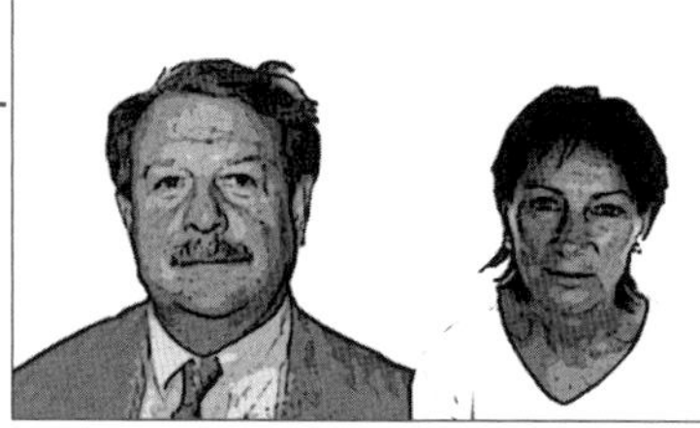

Escada Boutique [Paris [France [2000

Architects Anthony Béchu + Volume ABC [*Photographer* Fernando Javier Urquijo

Das deutsche Modelabel eröffnete seine französische Dependance in den alten Werkstätten eines französischen Couturiers mitten im Pariser Modedistrikt rund um die Avenue Montaigne. Es ist eine ehrfurchtgebietende Adresse und die Nachbarn hören auf so klangvolle Namen wie Chanel, Dior und Nina Ricci. Deshalb war das Konzept für den Laden klar: unbedingte Eleganz. Die Räume mit ihren gut 600 Quadratmetern atmen Großzügigkeit, Klarheit und Weite und können doch eine gewisse Nüchternheit nicht verleugnen. Doch hier gerät sie zur Tugend. Ein dezent in die Jahre gekommener, heller Naturstein aus dem Burgund, normalerweise als Straßenpflaster verwendet, bedeckt den Boden auf beiden Etagen und betont den urbanen Charakter der Einrichtung. Seidengepolsterte Wandverkleidungen, Edelhölzer, Lack und kühles Glas sowie zurückhaltende, pudrige Farben schaffen eine feine, sehr diskrete Atmosphäre, in der der Kunde edle Stoffe rascheln hört und den Geruch teuren Leders wahrnimmt. So mag man sich auf den modernen Sofas niederlassen und die Schönheit von puren Luxus genießen.

The German fashion label opened its French subsidiary in the old workshops of a French couturier in the middle of the Parisian fashion district around the Avenue Montaigne. It is an awe-inspiring address and the neighbours have such resonant names as Chanel, Dior and Nina Ricci. This is why the concept for the shop was clear: absolute elegance. The rooms, at least 600 square metres in area, breathe spaciousness, clarity and breadth, and cannot deny a certain sobriety. But here this becomes a virtue. A subtly aging, light natural stone from Burgundy, normally used as street plaster, covers the floor on both storeys and emphasises the urban character of the installation. Silk-padded wall coverings, rare woods, varnish, cool glass and reserved, powdery colours create a very fine, discrete atmosphere in which one hears noble fabrics rustling and smells the aroma of expensive leather. One can sit down on the modern sofas and enjoy the beauty of pure luxury.

Oben Kostbare Exponate: Schuhe und Taschen [*Above* Precious exhibits: shoes and handbags [*Rechts* Zurückhaltende Eleganz: Der Verkaufsraum [*Right* Reserved elegance: the sales room

ESCADA

Rechts Unaufdringlicher Charme: Deutsche Mode in Paris [*Right* Unobtrusive charm: German fashion in Paris

Links/Unten Die Inneneinrichtung dominieren pudrige, samtige Töne, leuchtende Akzente setzt die präsentierte Mode [*Left/Below* Powdery, velvety tones dominate the interior installation; the fashion being presented sets luminous accents

Florence Loewy Bookshop [Paris [France [2001

Architects Jakob + MacFarlane [*Photographer* Nicolas Borel

Es ist nur ein winziger Laden und doch der einzige in ganz Frankreich, der mit einem so wohlsortierten, ungewöhnlichen Sortiment an Kunst- und Designbüchern aufwarten kann. Das Geschäft mit seinen gerade mal 35 Quadratmetern benötigte eine neue innere Struktur und stand gleichzeitig vor der Herausforderung, den wachsenden Bücherbergen mit neuen Mitteln der Präsentation gerecht zu werden.
Entstanden ist eine Einrichtung, die mit ihren biomorph verformten Regalen fast selbst wie ein Kunstwerk aussieht. Für die Aufteilung der Fläche wurden die Bewegungen der Kunden in einem Buchladen studiert, die das Angebot betrachten, nach Büchern suchen und die Blicke schweifen lassen. Mutig wurde auf die üblichen Regalwände verzichtet und stattdessen ein Insel-Konzept verwirklicht, bei dem die Einbauten den Raum strukturieren. Diese Einbauten sind freilich mehr als bloße Raumteiler. Die Architekten nahmen das klassische Format eines Bildbandes, 360 Millimeter, zum Ausgangspunkt ihres Entwurfs und entwickelten mit diesem Maß dreidimensionale, surreal verzogene Konstrukte, die sich förmlich in den knapp bemessenen Raum an Wände und Decken schmiegen. Durch diesen Zuschnitt geben sie sich als speziell für Kunstbände entworfene Elemente zu erkennen, die sogar ein Innenleben haben. Denn mit ihrem hohlen Kern dienen diese Möbel gleichzeitig als Aufbewahrungs- und Lagerraum des Buchladens. Der Kunstband an sich beweist sich hier als Maß aller Dinge.

It is only a tiny shop, and yet the only one in all of France which can boast such a well-sorted, unusual assortment of art and design books. The business with its only 35 square metres required a new interior structure and immediately stood before the challenge of doing justice to the growing mountains of books and new means of presentation.
The result is an installation that almost looks like a work of art itself with its biomorphic-shaped shelves. The movements of the customers in a bookshop was studied to determine the distribution of the surfaces: how they studied what was being offered, searched for books and let their glances wander. The customary shelf-walls were courageously dispensed with and an island concept developed instead in which the installations structure the room. These installations are of course more than simply room partitions. The architects took the classical format of the picture-book, 360 millimetres, as the point of the departure of their design and developed three-dimensional, surrealistic dancing constructions with this scale that actually clung in the small room. They can be recognised right away as having been especially designed for art books, and even have an inner life. With their hollow core, these pieces of furniture simultaneously serve as storage room for the bookshop. The picture-book proves itself to be the measure of all things in this case.

Die 60er Jahre
Michael Asher

Lieu Commun Shop [Paris [France [2005

Architect Matali Crasset [*Photographer* Patrick Gries

Der Laden im Pariser Szeneviertel Marais ist ein gemeinsames Projekt von Produktdesignern, einer Architektin sowie einem Musiklabel. Allein die toxischen Farben und der etwas polierte Retrolook des Geschäfts signalisieren: Achtung, hier spricht der Zeitgeist! Das Angebot ist so bunt wie die Einrichtung: Kleidung, Accessoires, Möbel, CDs und Design-Schnickschnack. Es gibt keine Aufteilung der ganz in blassem Himmelblau gehaltenen Ladenfläche nach Produzenten oder Warensortiment – nein, alles verschmilzt zu einem verspielten Kosmos, in dem vor allem die Freude an schönen, farbigen Dingen zählt. Neben den ambitionierten Objekten wirken die biomorphen, an Bäume erinnernden Displays aus unbehandeltem Birkenholz fast wie eine naive Dekoration. Doch sie sind das eigentliche Funktionselement der Einrichtung: beliebig aufstellbar, sehr robust und je nach Bedarf als Raumteiler oder Kleiderstange zu verwenden. Sie verleihen der artifiziell aufgeladenen Atmosphäre die nötige Bodenhaftung und schaffen es, die laute, überreizte Welt des modischen Produktdesigns etwas zu beruhigen.

This shop in the trendy Parisian neighbourhood of Marais is the shared project of a product designer, an architect and a music label. Already the toxic colours and somewhat polished retro-look of the shop signalise: look out, the Zeitgeist is speaking here. The goods on offer are just as colourful as the installation: clothing, accessories, furniture, CDs, design knickknacks. There is no subdivision of the pale sky-blue shop surface according to manufacturer or ware assortment – no, everything blends together into a playful cosmos in which, above all, the joy of beautiful, colourful things counts. Alongside the ambitious objects, the biomorphic displays of natural birch wood, reminiscent of trees, have almost the effect of a naïve decoration. But these are in fact the actual functional element of the installation: they can be set up where you like, they are very robust and can be used either as room dividers or clothes racks as desired. They lend the artificially charged atmosphere the necessary grounding, also managing to somewhat calm down the loud, over-stimulated world of fashion product design.

Links Quietschbunt sind sowohl Inneneinrichtung als auch die angebotenen Artikel
Left Both the interior installation and articles on offer are multicoloured [*Oben* Drei-D-Visualisierung [*Above* 3-D visualisation

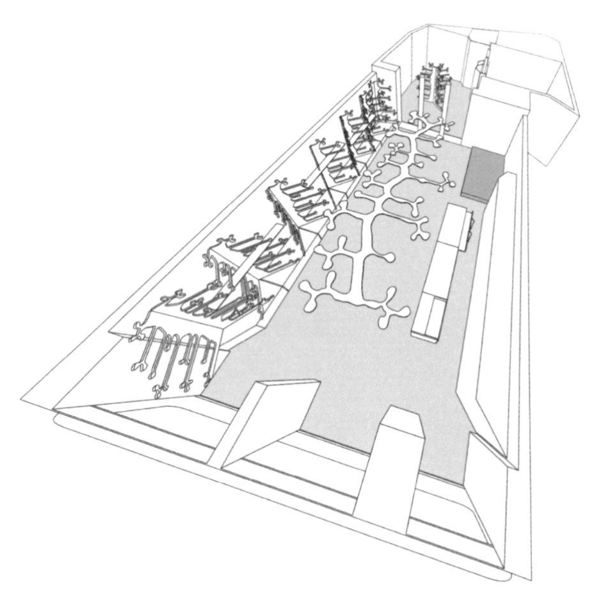

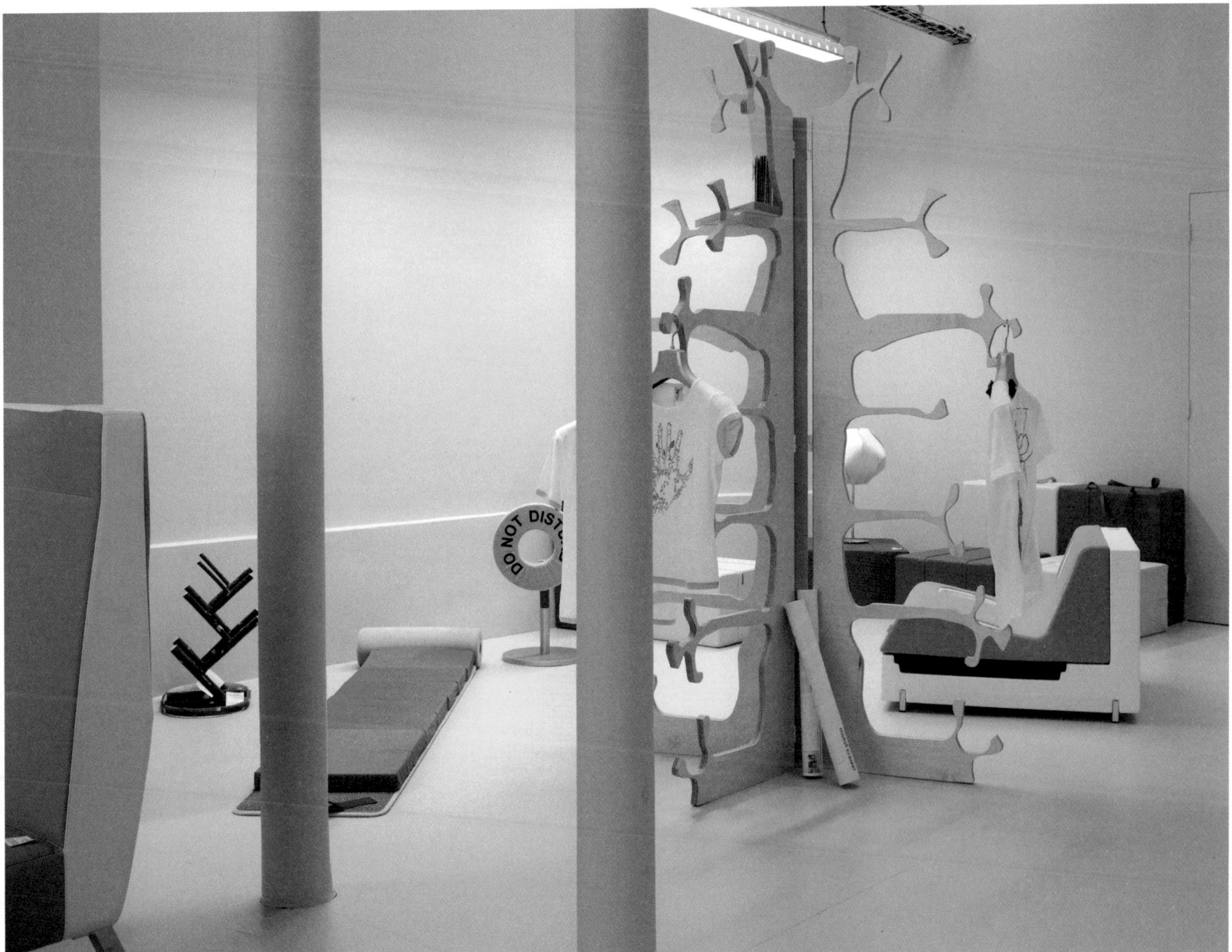

Casino [Basel [Switzerland [2003

Architect SM Design – Sybille de Margerie [*Photographer* Fabrice Rambert

Basel ist ein Ort der Kunst. Der modernen Kunst vor allem. Und so wundert es nicht, dass auch das örtliche Casino daran interessiert war, seinen Spielbetrieb mit ein paar Anleihen bei der Bildenden Kunst zu veredeln. Namentlich Jean Tinguely, der Bildhauer und Maler, dem auch ein Museum in der Stadt gewidmet ist, inspirierte den Entwurf für die Neugestaltung der Spielbank.

Schon das Äußere des Gebäudes räumt mit allen Erwartungen an ein klassisches Casino auf: Anstelle von Belle-Époque-Dekor erwartet den Besucher ein roter Glaskubus. Und diese Farbe dominiert auch das Innere, eine rauschhafte, explosive Melange aus Himbeer- und Purpurtönen, durchsetzt mit Zinnober, Karmin und Violett. Das Restaurant gibt sich nicht weniger bescheiden, dafür aber atmosphärisch noch etwas kontrollierter: Es herrschen metallische Töne, Silber und Gold vor, der Boden ist mit Naturholz versehen. Die Tischreihen verlaufen parallel zu einer Glasfront, vor der irisierende Vorhänge den Eindruck eines Wasserfalls entstehen lassen. Und überall finden sich Tinguely-Zitate: Mobiles, geschwungene, farbenfrohe Ornamente. Es ist ein Wunderland, eine sinnliche Herausforderung auf drei Etagen. Die Spielautomaten blinken und irgendwo heißt es: Rien ne va plus.

Basel is a city of art, especially modern art. It is therefore not surprising that the local casino was interested in ennobling its game operation with a few loans from the pictorial arts. Jean Tinguely, sculptor and painter, to whom a museum in the city is dedicated, inspired the design for the new formation of the gambling casino.

The exterior of the building already dispenses with any expectations of a classic casino – instead of Belle-Époque décor, the visitor is confronted with a red glass cube. This colour also dominates the interior: an intoxicating, explosive mixture of raspberry and purple tones, shot through with cinnabar, carmine and violet. The restaurant is no less modest but rather more controlled in terms of atmosphere. Here, metallic tones dominate, silver and gold, and the floor is of natural wood. The rows of tables run parallel to a glass front; in front of these, iridescent curtains give the impression of a waterfall. Tinguely quotations are everywhere: mobiles, curved, colourful ornaments. It is a wonderland, a sensual challenge on three storeys. The gambling machines flash, and somewhere it is said: Rien ne va plus.

Oben Faites vos jeux! Eingang zum Casinosaal [*Above* Faites vos jeux! Faites vos jeux! Entrance to the casino hall

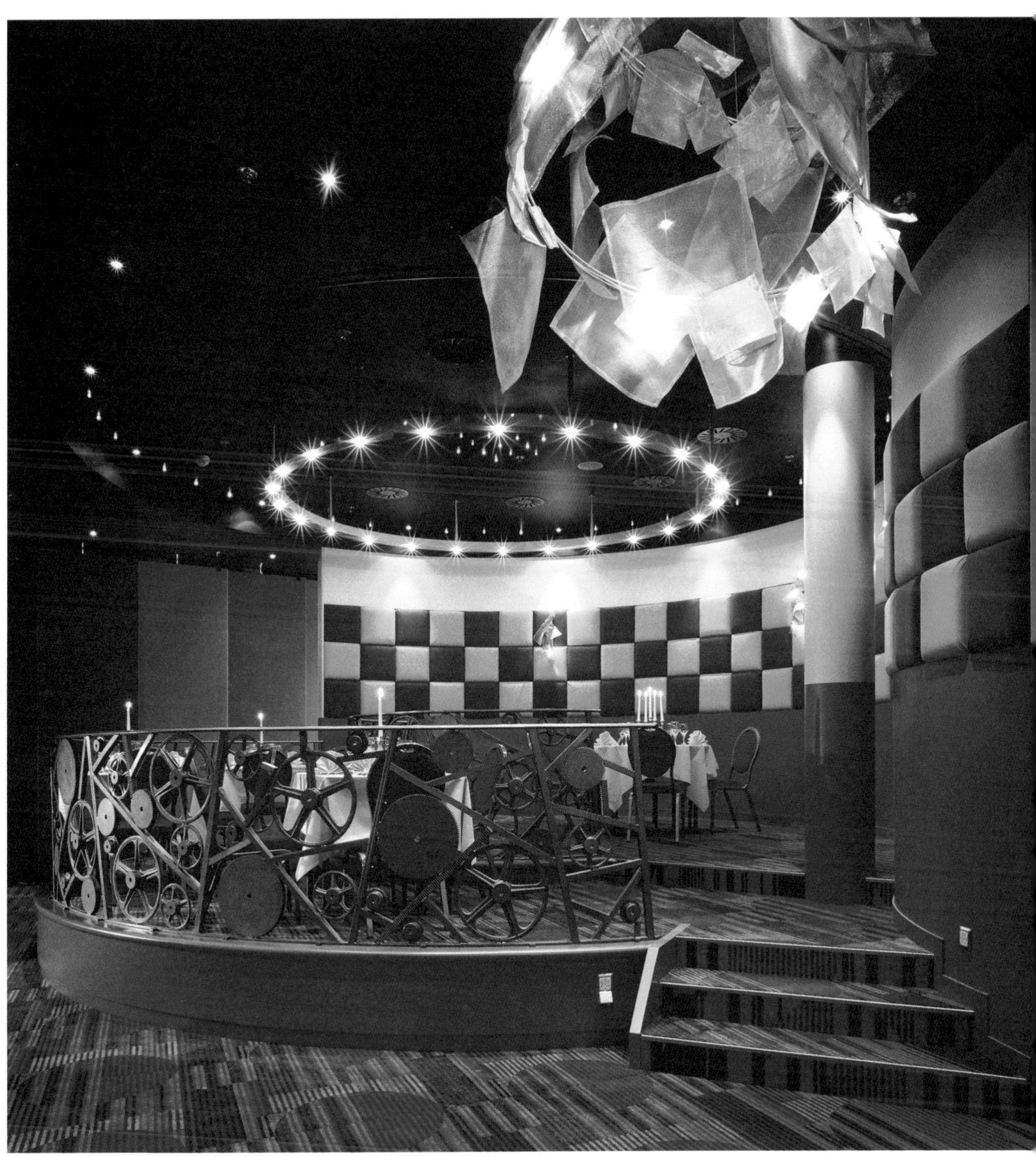

Oben Rot gewinnt: Restaurantbereich [*Above* Red wins: restaurant area

Links/Unten Die Kugel rollt: Der Kreis ist beherrschendes Motiv [*Left/Below* The ball rolls: the circle is the dominant motif [*Rechts* Barbereich [*Right* Bar area

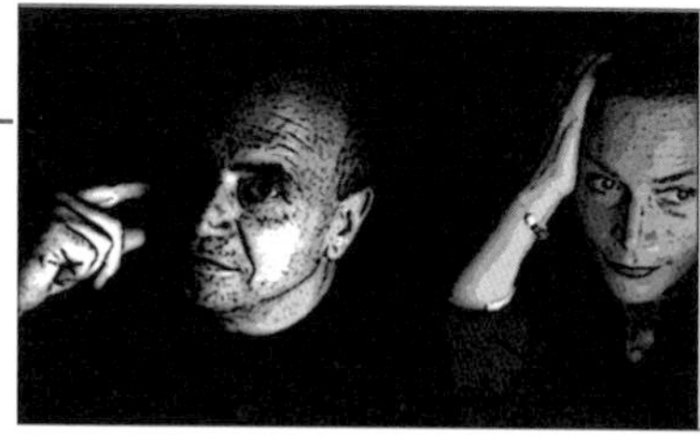

EA CAFFE in Emporio Armani [Hong Kong [China [2002

Architects Massimiliano + Doriana Fuksas [*Photographers* Ramon Prat, Maurizio Marcato

Diese Science-Fiction-Kulisse ist ernst gemeint. Sie ist ein Café. Und noch dazu eines, das zu einem fernöstlichen Vorposten abendländischer Konsumkultur gehört. Dabei hat man hierzulande so etwas noch nie gesehen. Direkt aus der angeschlossenen Edelboutique gelangt man in das Lokal und gerät unmittelbar in den Strudel eines knallroten Bandes aus Fiberglas. Nennen wir es Raumelement, denn seine Länge beträgt 105 Meter, seine Breite 0,7 Meter. Es handelt sich also um ein recht massives Stück Architektur. Aus dem hochglänzenden blauen Boden wachsend, entwickelt es sich in unregelmäßig auf- und absteigenden Drehbewegungen zu einer Bar, die sich allmählich in einen großen Imbisstresen verwandelt. Zwischendurch war dieses Element bereits ein DJ-Pult, das sich wiederum ein Stück weiter in eine Bar zurückbildet. Und irgendwann umwickelt dieses rote Ungetüm einen Restaurantbereich und läuft als begehbare Spirale auf den Ausgang zu. Sein »Gegenspieler« ist ein Lichtband in der azurblauen Decke, beide machen gemeinsame Sache. Sie strukturieren den Raum und verleihen ihm die Atmosphäre eines Space Shuttles. Die transparenten Wände können ihre Farbe je nach Tageszeit und Stimmung verändern, so dass alles hier keinen Bezug mehr zum realen Geschehen draußen hat. Doch muss die irdische Außenwelt noch jemanden interessieren? Die Besucher nehmen Platz auf dünnbeinigen Stahlstühlen mit einer halb durchsichtigen, seidigen Kunststoffoberfläche und dürfen ein Stück mitfliegen.

This science-fiction backdrop is intended seriously. It is a café; moreover, one that belongs to a Far Eastern outpost of occidental consumer culture. Still, people had never seen anything like this here before. One arrives in the cafe directly from the adjoining noble boutique and immediately lands in the maelstrom of a bright-red fibreglass band. Let's call it a room-element, for it is 105 metres long and 0.7 metres wide. It is therefore a real massive piece of architecture. It grows out of the shining blue, wooden floor and develops in irregularly ascending and descending rotations to a bar which is gradually transformed into a large snack counter. In between, this element was already a DJ stand that receded again into a bar a bit further on. Then, at some point, this red impetuosity winds round a restaurant area, running up to the exit in the form of a spiral that one can walk on. Its counterpart is a band of light in the azure-blue ceiling – both do the job together. They structure the room and lend it the atmosphere of a space-shuttle. The transparent walls can change their colour according to the time of day and mood, so that nothing here has any relationship to real events going on outside. But surely the earthly element still interests someone? The visitors take their seats on the thin-legged steel stools with a translucent, silk surface and can join the flight for a while.

Links Antagonisten aus Licht und Acryl [*Left* Antagonists out of light and acrylic [*Unten* Im Wendekreis des Cocktails: Barbereich [*Below* Tropic of Cocktail: bar area

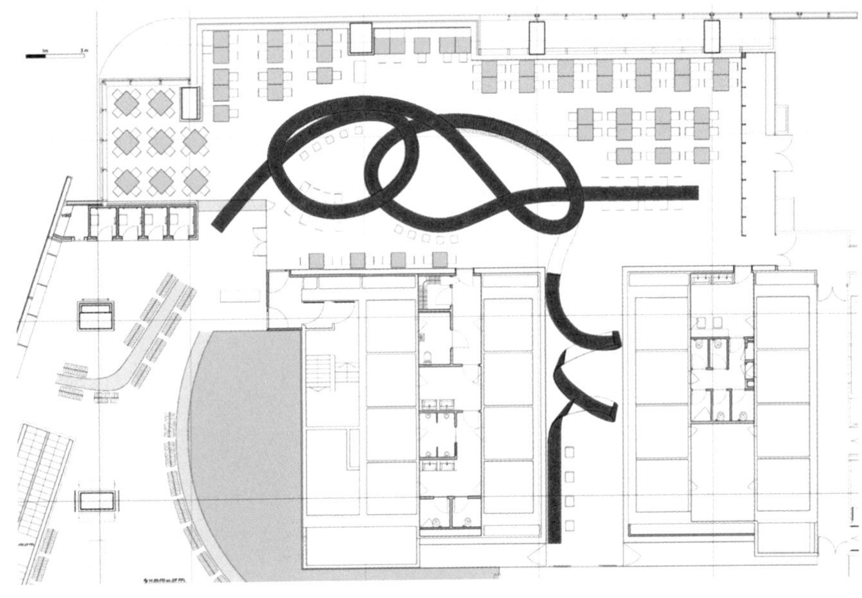

Le CAB – Club, Lounge, Bar [Paris [France [2003

Architect Ora-Ïto [*Photographer* Ora-Ïto

Das Lokal, ein Zwitterwesen aus Bar, Lounge und Club, spielt mit den traditionellen Chiffren gepflegter Erwachsenenunterhaltung. Kräftige, dunkel-satte Farben wie Bordeauxrot, nobles Material wie Leder und bequeme, weiche Polster erinnern an die guten Etablissements des städtischen Nachtlebens, doch hier verschmilzt dieses Déjà-vu mit neuen Elementen. Vor allem das Licht spielt eine dramaturgisch unverzichtbare Rolle in der modernen, keinesfalls modischen Inszenierung. Die Beleuchtung gibt der Architektur einen Rahmen, doch ihren eigentlichen Einsatz bekommt sie, wenn es um die Wahrnehmung der Gäste geht. Zwar dient das Licht auch der Orientierung – Lichtbänder auf dem Boden markieren die Tanzfläche – doch zusammen mit absichtsvoll platzierten Spiegeln und Glasflächen, kaschierten Leuchtbändern und den Dimensionen der Architektur werden irritierende Vexierbilder produziert, in denen sich die Besucher verlieren können. Die Farbe der Lichtquellen lässt sich ebenso steuern wie die Intensität, und so verwischen im Laufe einer Nacht die Grenzen zwischen Oben und Unten, Hell und Dunkel auf denkbar magische Art.

This hermaphrodite, a combination of bar, lounge and club, plays with the traditional signals of high-class adult entertainment. Powerfully dark, full colours such as Bordeaux red, fine materials like leather and comfortable, soft cushions remind one of the good establishments of urban night-life, but here this déjà-vu is mixed with new elements. Especially light plays a dramaturgically indispensable role in the modern, not at all trendy scenery. The lighting gives the architecture a framework, but its actual use is in perception of the guests. The light serves to orientate as well – light-bands on the floor mark the dancing surface – but irritating picture-puzzles are formed in which the visitors could get lost. These are formed by intentionally placed mirrors and glass surfaces, hidden light-bands and the dimensions of the architecture. The colour of the light-sources can be controlled, as can their intensity, and thus the boundaries between above and below, bright and dark are magically blurred during the course of the night.

Links/Unten Licht- und Farbeffekte sind wohldosiert und gekonnt inszeniert [*Left/Below* Lighting and colour effects are well-dosed and skilfully staged

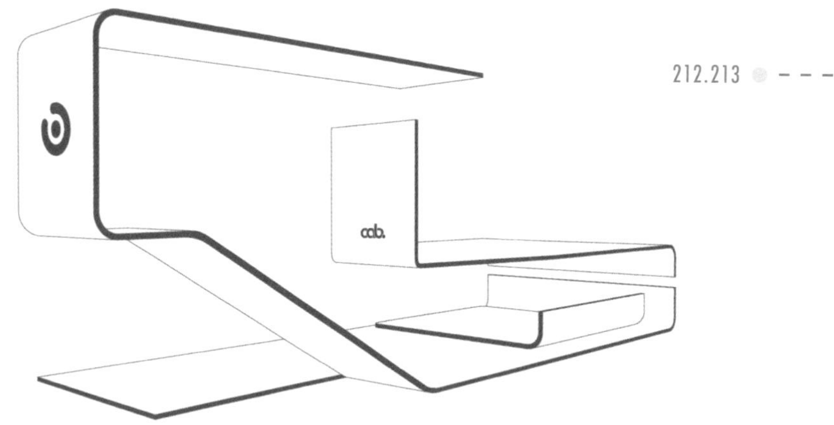
cab.

MIX – Restaurant and Bar [Las Vegas [USA [2004

Architect Patrick Jouin [*Photographers* Eric Laignel, Thomas Duval

Man muss nicht lange nach einer Metapher für die Gestaltungsidee dieser Lokalität suchen: Das Reich der Sünde und der Himmel waren schon immer aufeinander angewiesen. Diesem Einfall folgt die Gestaltung bis in die letzten Details. Wer aus dem Fahrstuhl tritt, befindet sich gleich in einer überdimensionalen Bar mit 300 Plätzen, über der ein feuerrot loderndes Korallenriff in den dunklen Himmel der Decke wächst. Schwarze Ledersessel mit einem gezackten Edelstahlsockel sind um runde, schwach hinterleuchtete Tische gruppiert. Im Inneren des Korallenriffs wurde ein sehr intimer Raum geschaffen, von dem aus die Besucher einen Panoramablick über den gesamten Barbereich genießen können. An der äußersten Ecke der Etage befindet sich eine Champagnerbar, die mit ihren cremeweißen, futuristischen Möbeln und Einbauten an die Ausstattung von frühen Science-Fiction-Filmen erinnert. Das Betreten des Restaurants gerät zu einer Sensation. Über eine Art Tunnel gelangt man in diesen Bereich, von dessen zehn Meter hoher Decke ein Lüster aus 15.000 Muranoglaskugeln bis fast auf den Boden hängt: ein himmlisches Glockenspiel. In Struktur und Gliederung so ähnlich wie die Bar gestaltet – auch hier gibt es eine intim gestaltete Zwischenetage im Zentrum –, umfängt die Besucher eine geradezu paradiesische Reinheit. Kein Zweifel, der Himmel ist von Las Vegas aus am besten zu erreichen.

One doesn't have to search long for a metaphor for the design idea of this locality: the realms of sin and of heaven have always depended on each other. The design follows this idea right up to the final details. When you leave the lift, you immediately find yourself in an over-dimensional bar with 300 seats, above which a fire-red blazing coral-reef grows in the black sky of the ceiling. Black leather easy-chairs with indented stainless-steel bases are grouped around slightly illuminated tables. An intimate space has been created on the inside of the coral-reef from which visitors can enjoy a panoramic view over the entire barroom. A champagne bar is situated on the outermost corner of the storey, reminiscent of early science-fiction scenery with its creamy white, futuristic furniture and installations. Entering the restaurant is a real sensation. One enters this area through a kind of tunnel; a chandelier of 15,000 Murano glass-balls hangs from the 10-metre-high ceiling almost to the floor – a heavenly glockenspiel. It is similar to the bar in structure and distribution – there is an intimately designed in-between storey in the centre as well – the visitor is surrounded by a purity almost like paradise. There is no doubt about it – heaven can best be reached from Las Vegas.

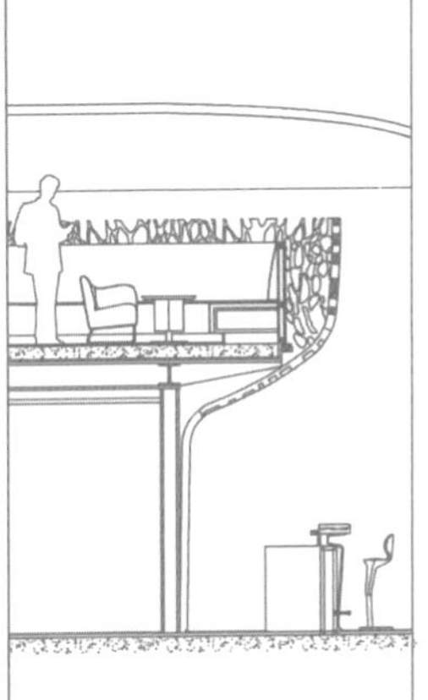

Oben Schönes Laster: Die Bar [*Above* Beautiful vice: the bar
Rechts Details [*Right* Details

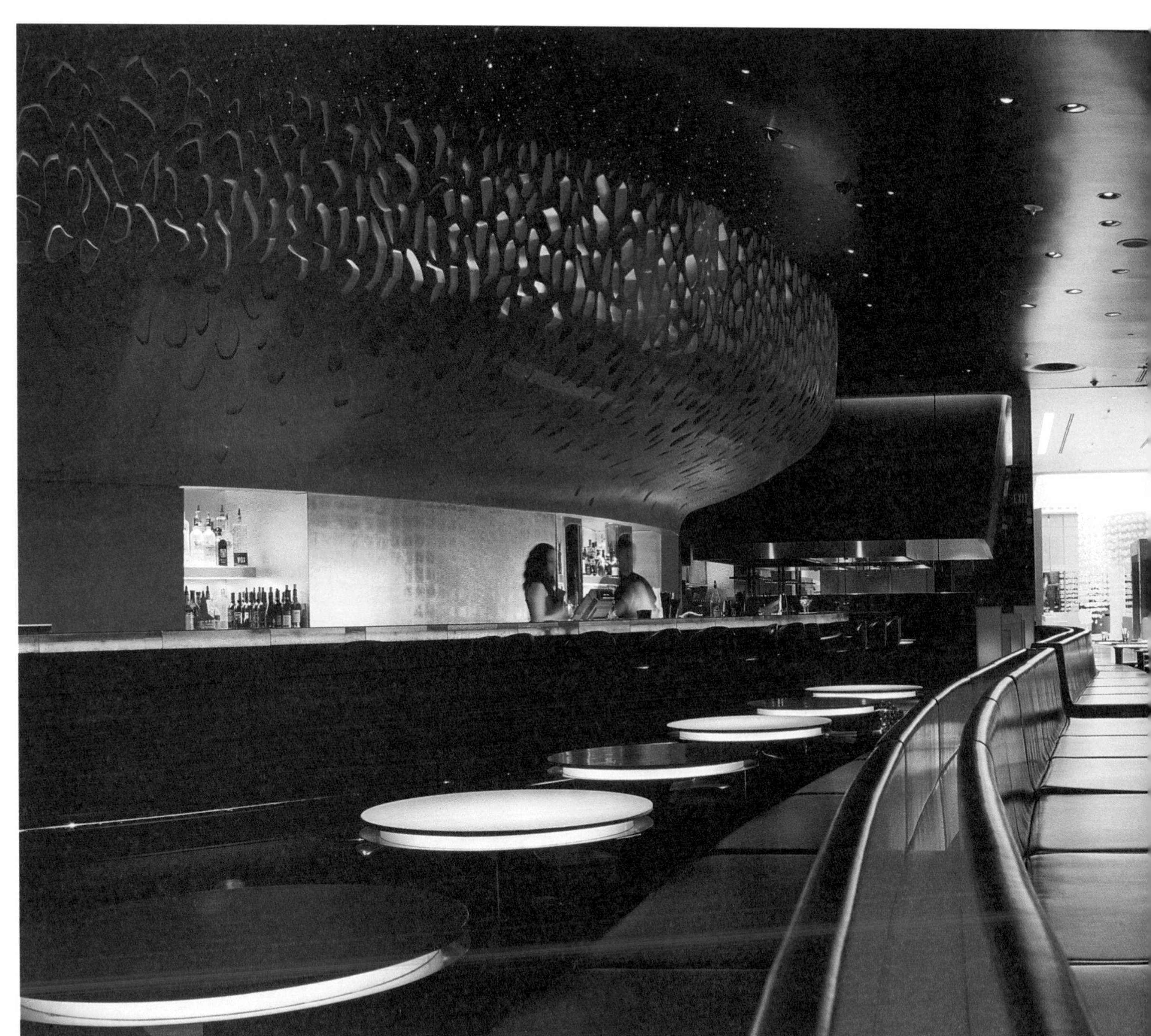

Oben Die Unterwelt: Blick in den Barbereich [*Above* The underworld: view into the bar area

Oben Überirdisch: Das Restaurant mit dem fantastischen Lüster aus unzähligen Muranoglaskugeln [*Above* Heavenly: the restaurant with its fantastic chandelier out of innumerable Murano glass spheres

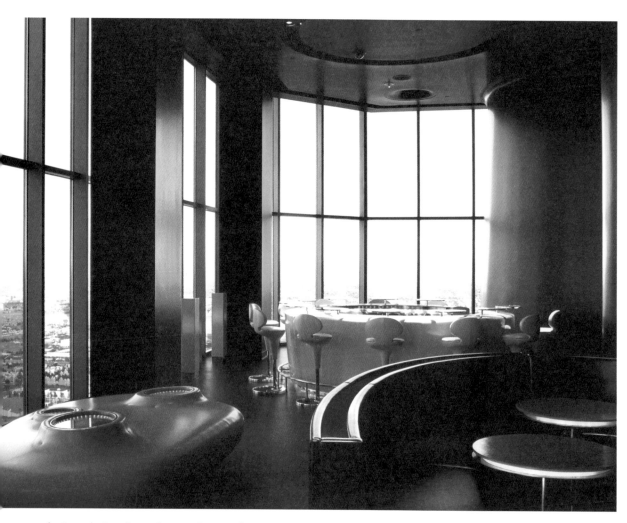

Oben Kosmische Konstellation: Champagnerbar [*Above* Cosmic constellation: Champagne bar [*Unten* Schnitt Restaurant [*Below* Section restaurant

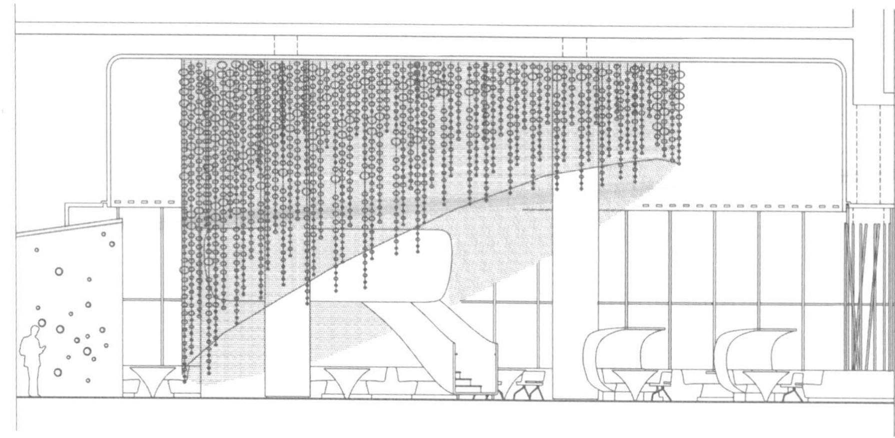

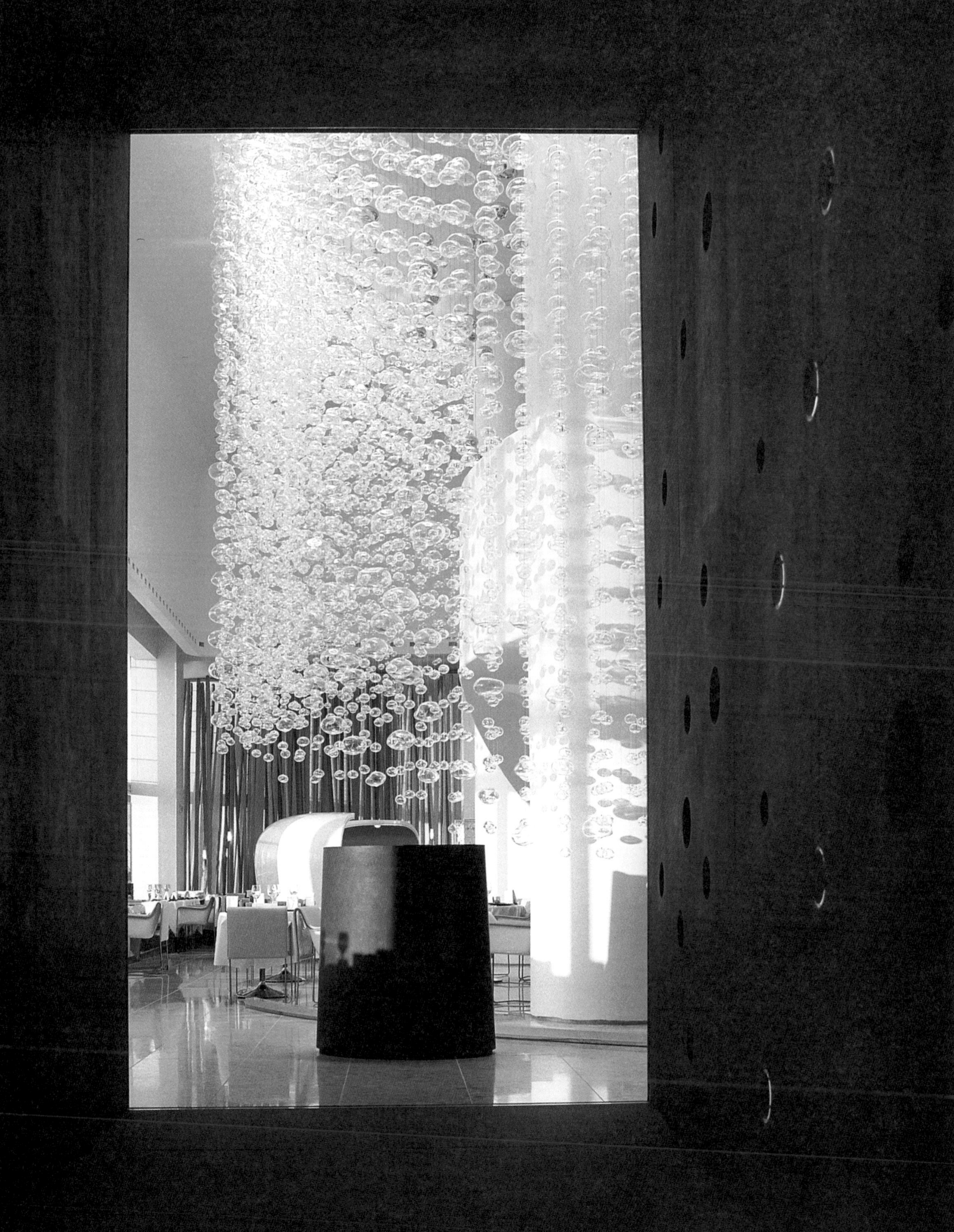

impressum

Die Deutsche Bibliothek verzeichnet diese Publikation in der *Deutschen Nationalbibliografie*. Detaillierte bibliografische Daten sind im Internet über *http://dnb.ddb.de* abrufbar.
Die Deutsche Bibliothek lists this publication in the *Deutsche Nationalbibliografie*; detailed bibliographic data is available on the internet at *http://dnb.ddb.de*.

ISBN 978-3-938666-31-9

www.dom-publishers.com

Lektorat Uta Keil [*Übersetzung* Cord von der Lühe, Berlin

Grafische Gestaltung Susanne Weigelt, Leipzig